ONE WOMAN'S TRUE
LIFE STORY oF HOPE

Survivor

JANE FARACO

Editorial development and creative design support by Ascent:
www.itsyourlifebethere.com

ISBN: 978-1-09484-175-5
Printed in the United States of America

 JaneFaraco | @JaneFaraco | www.WeSurviveWeThrive.com

"There is no greater agony than bearing an untold story inside you."

— MAYA ANGELOU

One thing I knew for sure when putting pen to paper is that as I sought the courage to reveal *my* truth, I vowed that in telling *my* story, I would do my best not to hurt anyone in the process. I hope I have succeeded. Some of the names have been changed, timelines adjusted, circumstances altered for the sake of kindness and anonymity.

—Jane

Thank You

THANK YOU to my husband, Jim, for all of your amazing support during my writing journey. I so much wanted and needed to tell *my* story but how would I do it without revealing yours as well. Married for many years now, our lives and our stories are completely intertwined and yet, 'each child has his own.' I love you and thank you for giving me your complete 'go ahead' on this book. I never would have done this without it.

Thank you David Hazard, my very direct but gentle writing coach. I could not have written my memoir without you. When we met, I knew within just a few moments that you would 'get' my story. Thank you also for your intuition and understanding of what I was trying to say even when I wasn't really sure myself. Thank you for your encouragement

7

and your schedule which kept me on track. Thank you for influencing me with your spirituality which guided me to keep on writing at times when the only thing I had was the hope that perhaps the book might in some way help someone.

Thank you to book designer Peter Gloege for creating a very intriguing cover and beautifully simple illustrations for SURVIVOR.

Thank you to my dear friend, author Jeanne Selander Miller who, after reading some of my writings, convinced me that I had a story to tell and the ability to tell it.

Many thanks to my wonderful beta readers who provided me with much needed corrections, input and perspective and thank you for your ongoing encouragement and support in writing this very personal memoir: Sherry Hickman, Sheila Halpin, Judy Zipkin Grasso, Susan Hazard Rimato, Don and Carolyn Evers, Julie Peters, PJ Layng, Priscilla MacDougall, Laurie Stewart, Barbara Crutchfield, Annie Smith, Alma Phipps, Sarah Norkus, Patricia Kurman, Sarah Milstead, Bill Ludwick and Kathy D'Amelio.

The Process

MORE THAN SIX MONTHS after thinking Survivor was complete, I was haunted. This was to be a tell-all personal expose, but was it really? Something was missing but what? At first I couldn't put my finger on it. Even after submitting my final edit to David, my writing coach, I still felt shot through with sad empty holes like the secretive Swiss cheese I had become.. After all, I'd carefully tippy toed around everyone in my life and shared with others only a conjured up version of what seemed like an acceptable reality. My writing, although revealing remained stilted. I thought, 'is everything forever going to be a secret.'

After all I'd had secrets in my sexuality, childhood and marital secrets and I felt I was expected to maintain them. So, this has been anything but easy.

My life was a locked door to a secret room. Searching for the key has been a lifelong endeavor. It creaked when first opened, then, stuck, it opened an inch or two. The creaking ceased, the opening enlarged, eventually swinging wide open. And then, even more more was to be revealed. The picture has become crystal clear. I now share with you *everything.**

---

* Well, almost everything . . . Survivor takes place from 1946 to 1987—until age 41

Chapter 1

IT WAS 1950 and I was just four when we left London for New York aboard the illustrious Queen Mary, the most exciting thing ever, or nearly anyway. I would soon discover something much more exciting than a cruise on this luxury liner.

My mother was beside herself at the thought of the grandeur. She looked forward to dressing for romantic dinners in the beautiful dining room and dancing after.

She waxed ecstatic, "Oh, the Queen Mary, we are taking the *Queen Mary*."

Mommy had me almost crazy with wonder and anticipation. I wondered just how large this ship would be, how many cabins. She said it was enormous, fancy and had many decks. Mother, Daddy, Granny and I would be on-board for days, actually living on the ship.

'Who else would be on board? Would I make friends?'

The Queen had been stripped down and converted into a troop ship during World War II. Those voyages had been *sans* the usual chic travelers, haute cuisine and ballroom dancing. After the war, she was revamped for cruise service and grand once again. With her polished decks, dining rooms with crystal chandeliers, formal service and beautiful state rooms, it had all the pomp my mother required and a nightly cocktail party scene; the parents were all in on that and for my aging Granny and me, a comfortable suite with all the amenities.

Even with all of this excitement, I was remarkably bored for a four year old. I had my own idea of ship-board fun. This small child was driven by an unstoppable curiosity, *and something else. . .*

The ship had just left port on our journey when my parents suddenly realized I was missing. They and Granny had carelessly turned their backs while boarding the ship and *just like that,* I had slipped away. Looking for an out, I escaped. Panic ensued. 'Was I back in port? Had I fallen in or was I somewhere on the ship?'

Running along the deck, hair ribbons trailing behind me, the breezes were delicious, tasting like freedom.

I scampered through a beautiful dining room with its gleaming silverware and pretty flowers and found my way out another door, back onto a different deck. I wondered where the dark gray metal steps led. Without the least bit of caution, down I went. It was scary, but fun. I hadn't ventured out on my own much before, I'd been *so* under their thumb. Down one deck and then some more, I arrived where the sailors lived, all gray and white walls with lots of handsome black-and white-uniformed sailors rushing around.

One caught my eye. "Well, hello there, young lady. Who have we here?"

Feeling the need to explain I told him, "I'm here with my parents. I wanted to see what's down here."

"OK then, let's go to the break room. Do you want some juice?"

It was warm down there and the break room smelled of coffee and sandwiches. My new sailor friend, a couple of others and I had a little chat. One of them gave me a magazine, another pulled out some paper and pencils.

"Thank you." I said and I started to draw. When I tired of that, I paged through the magazine. A call must have been made to let the right people know they'd captured a small passenger. Captured or not, I felt free.

Meanwhile, my parents had located the ship's authorities, who phoned ashore to determine I had *not* been left behind. Now, after a long search, my mother, who was beside herself, arrived along with my father and one of the ship's officers. There I was, looking at a magazine with my new sailor boys, when my parents suddenly burst into the room.

"Hello, Mommy. Hello, Daddy."

My mother hid her fury behind her cool exterior while my father calmly thanked the sailors and then turned to me.

"Honey you've given us quite a scare. How very independent you are," accompanied by a big warm hug.

And so began our cruise to New York and also another type of journey, one I would be on the rest of my life. My adventure *alone* down into the depths of the Queen Mary was just my *first* escape from the confines, rules and restrictions of the adult world in which I lived. It gave me my first taste of an independence I craved, even at that very young age.

A couple of years later, while hiding on the landing at the top of the stairs to the living room, I would hear my parents gaily retell this story while enjoying cocktails with friends and I'd wonder:

'Who let's go of the hand of a four-year-old boarding a ship? Who fails to notice she's gone until almost too late?' By then I understood exactly the kind of parents I had: the kind who could lose track of child.

My parents who were both from upstate New York, met in 1944 in London during the War. Daddy, who was in the Army and my mother, in the Red Cross married a year later. After the end of the war, Daddy took a consignment with an American company, first in Stockholm and later in Brussels where I was conceived and from that time on they embarrassingly referred to me as their 'souvenir of the war' or embarrassingly enough, a nickname, 'Souvey' for short.

Now we were to be living back in the States, in the Midwest, where Daddy was sent on a business assignment, Peoria, Illinois, to be exact, of 'it won't play well in Peoria' fame.

Mother found it impossible to imagine herself living in the droll Midwest after spending her twenties working in Manhattan and living in Europe for the last few years. She and my father had loved their European life. We spoke only French at home. Ah yes, we were quite the cosmopolitan family.

My rather fancy mother who looked like Joan Crawford and spoke with a WASPY high tone lilt much like Julia Child, was a more than, extremely proud descendant of the prominent Hudson Valley, Livingston family. The Livingston's claimed two signers of the Declaration of Independence, a

Chancellor of France, an arranger of the Louisiana Purchase, governors, judges, land barons, and gentlemen farmers who, at one time, owned more than 600,000 acres in upstate New York. Mother took ancestral pride to a new level. These were strong people with an aristocratic lineage, an astute business ethic, absolutely no nonsense, and the great possibility of being *entirely* humorless. They were stringent people, Dutch Reform, fire and brimstone and these attitudes remained in the generations that followed.

I remember 'the big house' in Clermont, NY, Columbia County where my grandmother lived. It was all about family history and the huge and very beautiful white clapboard farmhouse filled with the most interesting things. The furniture had been in the same position for hundreds of years. The house was complete with ancestral portraits, coats of arms, an old, almost life size wood rocking horse, a curiously weird but beautiful stuffed white snow owl, original old stone kitchens, horsehair sofas and comfy, old four poster beds. I could have stayed forever. My uncle farmed the apple orchard and tended to the chickens, a few goats and sheep-while tenants managed the rest of the property-a gentleman's farm for sure with lineage and bragging rights.

My lawyer/judge grandfather had managed the farm before that. All the beauty and all the pride in her family couldn't keep Mother on the farm. Her new life after college at Simmons in Boston would be lived in New York. She had moved on and had become a New Yorker. So, it was impossible for Mother to imagine herself in the rural Midwest after having already escaped the family Apple Orchards in the Hudson Valley.

The farmhouse Daddy rented for us in the States wasn't actually in Peoria but at least twenty miles outside, in a remote farm area, called Gardena.

Completely horrified with our new digs, Mommy said, "Well, it's come to this. Now we live in the godforsaken boondocks."

Peoria, Illinois—not cultured, not sophisticated, in the middle of the "damned corn belt," where "the corn was only fit for pigs." That's what she said anyway.

However, the City of Peoria looked like New York compared to Gardena. The house was not only on a remote country road but we only had one car and my father needed it for work. Stuck. She was stuck at home with me. A fate worse than death it seemed.

I am quite sure having babies wasn't Mother's thing. She later said she was uncomfortable with it. "How do you even talk to a baby?" Later I would hear," I couldn't hold a conversation with her until she was almost fourteen." She was far too sophisticated to possibly play with a child, the mundane day to day routine of it. She was trapped. So it seemed, was I.

I eagerly sought out the new neighbors, who farmed the land. They had a bunch of scrappy kids who cursed and did whatever they wanted. We'd run around their garden picking big, warm, sun-ripened tomatoes, eagerly sprinkling them with salt shakers before devouring them. Their mother made macaroni and cheese for dinner in a big, old, heavy black pan while dishes piled up in the sink and their crazy dogs ran around in circles in the kitchen. Complete mayhem. We all wailed with laughter. I was crazy for it. I loved the chaos. These people fascinated me.

Not long after we'd settled in, I'd once again gone missing. I'd found new friends, the workmen who'd been hired for a project at the neighbors barn. Joining them every day on their lunch break, the guys and I would sit on the grass with our backs leaning against the barn while eating lunch. Buddies, I had buddies. It was with them I learned how to drink soda out of a bottle. They howled with laughter as I put the whole opening of the bottle in my mouth.

"No, no, you just put this part of your mouth on it, like this."

And so I learned the right way to drink soda out of a bottle. I wasn't allowed soda at home so this was amazingly cool. Mother wasn't in the least impressed with my new soda drinking skills and she was super mad when she found me hanging with the guys on the other side of the barn. The workers appeared every morning for a couple of weeks and I was crushed when they stopped coming. These guys knew things. I'd hoped they were going to be my new best friends. So disappointed, I'd thought they were mine for a while. Losing them was just my first taste of the impermanence of things.

We'd been settled in the house for almost six months when my Uncle Ed, (my mother's brother), and his wife, Aunt Betty, (neither of whom had met me or my father), were to come for a week with my little cousins, Harold and Marshall. 'A week of fun,' I gleefully thought. 'I have cousins, family.'

I remember this like it was yesterday. My father had been warned.

"Jack, please don't drink while they are here."

Apparently, earlier, Ed had also given Betty, his Irish, fun loving, bit of a wild card wife, a rather stern warning. But after they arrived, Jack took one look at Betty and saw in her a drinking buddy and from that point on they had plans of their own. I'm not sure exactly what happened but they partied loudly and into the wee hours while the rest of us tried to sleep. I couldn't sleep at all that night but it wasn't just the excitement of looking forward to a fun week that kept me up. I nervously tucked myself deep into my bed, covering my head with quilts. What was happening? At first it was the laughter, then nervous arguing, followed by the yelling and slamming of doors. My day that had started with such fun had ended in a scary sleepless night.

The next morning was rocky to say the least. It seemed everyone was angry. Ed and Betty were screaming. Betty was a mad as hell, hot mess, slurring her words while my father was in a horrible drunken rage. Harold, Marshall and I were crying and my horribly embarrassed mother was scurrying around making an attempt to pick up the pieces. Their first night with us had been too unbearable for Ed, really for all of us.

By morning, Ed attempted to regain control while packing their things. He wasn't having even one more moment of their nonsense. The much anticipated visit ended abruptly with Ed, Betty and their children making a hasty retreat.

After they left, daddy stumbled into the living room and onto the sofa, dominating the living room like the elephant that he surely was, as though nothing had happened.

Stunned by the events that developed between our relatives' joyous arrival and their eventual escape, it had become painfully obvious to me that something had radically changed in my house. Daddy's drinking wasn't as innocent as it seemed, and I now saw that mother must have had good reason for being upset with him most of the time. I was embarrassed, so embarrassed and so sad. How could my father have ruined the much anticipated family visit. I couldn't imagine a thing like this happening. How much I wanted to play with my cousins but that wasn't to be. He had ruined everything.

You know it wasn't just my father, it was Betty too. There was something between them. I wouldn't call it hanky panky but I would say that they had an instant rapport that made them want to hang out together while the rest of us were expected leave them alone and pretend it wasn't happening. They had a sort of 'us against them attitude,' like bad children hiding from the rest, doing what they wanted despite the consequences. I get it now, as an adult I've behaved similarly. I've been there myself. I know what it is.

The next day, I'd never seen my mother so upset. She wanted to be alone, but I was afraid. Daddy had gone off to a bar. I didn't know how to help her or even myself get over these crushed feelings. Crushed? I was devastated. Two things had happened, it seemed. I'd discovered some sad truths about my father, about how his drinking could bring on such chaos and upset everyone; how powerful it was and how family members whom I'd never met would be affected in such a way that it would send them packing.

And I learned something about my mother as well.

All I wanted to do later that morning was hang out in the house with my mother until I felt safe and all had returned to normal. I didn't know then but I could have hung in there for thirty two years till the day Daddy died and not a damn thing would have changed, nor would I feel safe. She sat in the living room reading a magazine, so I went outside to play and just as I closed the door, I heard the click of the front door locking. My mother had locked me out.

Stunned, I stared at the door in disbelief.

"Don't lock me out. I want to come back in. I want to be with you."

I knocked and knocked, "Please, *no,* don't lock me out."

"Why can't I come in?"

I can't tell you just how long I stood there begging,

"Mommy, let me in"

Crying, she screamed, "Stay out there."

That door remained locked till early evening, I was heartbroken and again, crushed. I couldn't understand why she wouldn't want me around her. My heart ached... Mothers were supposed to want to be with you. This was the beginning of my realizing I was in this thing, this chaos, alone.

After a year, our lease was over at the farm and it was time to find a new house in Peoria. I followed Mother through a few houses and then a larger, prettier one, watching her eye everything carefully, critically. If she didn't approve, the search would have continued, but she made her pronouncement;

"This house is *perfect*."

It had all the elements she required; a screened porch, fireplaces, big bedrooms. In fact, the house seemed like the perfect set up for a nice, "friggin" life, or so one might think. It was a lovely, red brick house, built in 1925 on a beautiful tree lined court. Once settled in, it was clear we were just a little different from the rest. Midwesterners in the Fifties knew what they liked and what they didn't and everything else seemed strange or weird to them.

The house was in St. Mark's Parish, at a time when Catholics referred to their neighborhood by parish rather than by section. My parents sent me to Catholic school, as was the tradition in my father's Irish Catholic family. On my first day of kindergarten at Saint Mark's, Sister Anne Marie asked my name;

"Souvey." I said.

"Souvey, I thought your name was Jane."

I wondered why she asked if she already knew. And then

I parroted my mother's grand voice in full affect. "Yes, my real name is Souvenir or Souvey for short. You see I was *conceived* in Brussels. *I* am their Souvenir of the War." Sister Anne Marie blinked. With more information about me than she ever wanted to know, she looked less than amused.

"Nevertheless, here at St. Mark's, we will call you Jane."

I could see even then with my little five-year-old eyes that so very much about us was wrong and we were not going to play well in Peoria.

"What does "conceived in Brussels" mean anyway?" I later asked my mother.

From then on I was caught in a clash between Mother and her high-toned ideas and mannerisms, her disapproval of all things Midwestern and the world we'd parked ourselves in, where the likes of Sister Anne Marie and Midwestern decorum ruled. When I brought up almost any experience from my personal life, like the fact that Mother had made us Aubergine D'Auvignon for dinner. . . or that my father travelled to Africa and Saudi Arabia once a year. . . or that I spoke French before I spoke English. . . I would hear what I came to call "the Midwest Mantra."

"I never heard of that."

As though never having heard of something meant it couldn't possibly exist or be valid. And so, it was between these two worlds that I came to understand I would need to stop acting like a tiny copy of my mother and develop my own shtick. More than that, since Mother dug her heels in against "droll" Midwestern living, I would have to find my own way. That would mean facing down another formidable force, Daddy.

Daddy had been a fun drinker who was before my eyes becoming a *very* serious drunk. He'd more often than not disappear into the local bars on two, three, and four-day binges making my mother crazy and me, scared. Our house was drenched with fear during Dad's bouts of drinking, lots of fear.

Mother, whose face would cloud with anxiety, seemed incapable of doing anything to alter his behavior. Angry words flew, but changed nothing. We lived on a knife-edge, wondering what was going to happen for both of us.

There were the good days with my father as well, when he was, as my mother put it, "on the wagon." These were the times when he seemed to be happy and himself. I didn't have to worry and yummy things would happen. I was a chubby child and like Daddy, I loved to eat. In fact, he and I had an eating thing going on, much to my mother's dismay. When my dad was sober, it was our ritual to shop at Peoria's only fancy food store, Benny Schwartz', before coming home to cook together. Daddy loved Benny. He was Jewish and from New York and they could relate.

Daddy really loved to bake. A big man in his jumbo apron—pans and bowls flying, chocolate drippings on the table and mixer blades just begging to be licked, he was having the time of his life. Really, he loved to eat.

Once, when I was eight, he outdid himself and threw his energies into creating the most delicious chocolate cake he'd ever attempted. The layers of dark chocolate cake emerged steaming from the oven to cool and topped with a yummy, creamy, chocolate frosting. When they were ready, he took great care to stack and frost them beautifully and with finesse.

That sweet thing full of love and beauty sat on the kitchen counter, the coveted object of my desire. How I wanted to dive right in. The problem was, between that gorgeous cake, the promise of deliciousness and me stood dinner and more formidable than that. . . my mother.

Finally, after the agony of a dreary, wordless 'only child,' parentally stressed out dinner, we were to have a piece. On a plate in front of me, there lay a gingerly-cut, thin slice, served by my practically anorexic mother. I stared. It was simply not enough for this budding overeater.

Licking the fork when my plate was empty, I wanted

more. When my parents settled in the living room and the coast was clear, I slipped quietly into the kitchen, thrilled that the cake had been left out.

On the counter was the knife.

In my head, however, dwelled the invisible barrier, the image of mother and her unhappy and disapproving grimace whenever I wanted something she didn't want me to have. I knew exactly how she would react if she knew I'd had more cake. My body was supposed to be taking on the same sylph-like appearance she had, but it definitely wasn't.

'Mother? Or cake?' Hmmm?

I reached for the huge, French knife she'd used to cut the cake. Paper thin slice by paper thin slice, I whittled that thing down by at least two servings, enjoying every scrumptious, forbidden bite. The living room chatter told me I was safe to continue my daring mission. In a few minutes, still slicing, I realized I had made the cut-open wedge *entirely* too large. Mother would know, like somehow she always knew when I'd slipped around her regulations, which I must admit, was often.

Panicking, I grabbed the entire cake with my chubby, little hands and squeezed it closed, until it looked like only the original, small wedge had been cut, making the diameter of the cake *unbelievably* smaller.

Maybe no one would notice. At this point, I wasn't even hungry but it had become a challenge to get away with removing as much as I could. Taking the knife again, I started to cut very thin horizontal slices across the bottom. Not just one, but another and another. The cake was now about two inches shorter, with the middle frosting line almost down to the plate. I had masterfully and finally engineered my desired portion.

"Yikes." Her shrill voice startled me from behind.

"Souvenir, ye gods." Mother nearly screamed. "What has happened to the cake?"

I turned to face her, thinking, 'You're not going to decide how big my portion is going to be. I got what I wanted.' I might have just told her, "I was hungry for God's sake!" But that was not the full truth. I was craving something and it wasn't cake. I was filling a deep and painful hole and to me cake was nurturing. For all the many ways he neglected us, my father's simple act of baking something nice was generous and kind. In contrast, and I knew it even then, my Mother was neglectful, with a tight fisted, withholding attitude.

Since there wasn't a lot of nurturing happening, I began to take on the task of nurturing myself. I was looking for peace, a sweet place where I could reside. I would take what I needed—even if that meant crossing boundaries. No, I would not be controlled by the *one person* who failed to nurture me.

I would reach for what I needed in life. God, it's no wonder

I wanted to escape.

Wordless, then, I said nothing, I could only stare back

at her as she regaled me about sneaking food and getting fat.

Only later would the words form in my mind: 'Mommy, I'm

not like you, thin and powerless, don't you get it? One day

you will see me no more.'

"I ain't lookin' for you to feel like me

See like me or be like me.

All I really want to do

Is baby, be friends with you"

— BOB DYLAN

Chapter 2

THE PROBLEMS in my house became even clearer to me around the age of six. No longer was I delightfully exploring the breezy decks of the Queen Mary. A new reality was beginning to settle in. My house wasn't remotely like the others.

There seemed to be a peace in the other kid's houses, honestly, a lack of shame. They seemed to live in 'front porch, screen door slamming, PJs at night, bedtime story, hot chocolate houses.

So much had changed in my little life since we returned to the States. Daddy's benders were becoming a regular thing. Mommy worried more while I became a conscious human being, not necessarily a good thing. I was so much more aware of what was going on around me. Some children go into denial when things are bad. In retrospect I wish I'd done so but the problems were too big, too real. My little life was shot through with secrets and pain. The nice house we had bought turned out to be one that looked good on the outside but had dark secrets inside. Good looking red brick facades can hide many a secret and truth be told, even by age seven; I hated my house, my life, daddy's drinking, the way he acted and of course, my mother for not rescuing me. I could see I was all alone on this journey and I was sinking fast, an only child whose life was focused on her father's three or four day weekly binge drinking and the problems that went along with it.

Daddy's benders took him to the Peoria bars. He had his favorites; local gin mills, (corner bar kind of places with old beer stained wood floors, red leather bar stools, faded mirrors, huge jars of pickled eggs and pig's feet and always the company of a bartender willing to chat or commiserate.) I know these things because he'd take me with him regularly. . . until one evening when I was about seven. Now I don't remember the details of the evening but Daddy and I were dropped off by a taxi some time just before midnight. Mother was seethingly furious and I was never allowed to accompany him again.

As strange as it was, this going to the bar with my father and wondering what the appeal for him was in just sitting on that barstool and drinking, I loved it. I got lots of attention and all the snacks and Orange Crush I could handle.

After I wasn't going anymore, he opted for someone else to go with him with him on his bar hopping forees—*the dog*. I remember being *highly insulted*. I thought, 'Really? Am I equal to the dog as far as good company goes? The dog can't even *talk*.'

'What the heck,' I thought,' I am being replaced by the darn dog.'

Daddy went to fancy cocktail bars too, one called the Sazerac, named after the most famous drink of New Orleans. The Sazerac had a steady stream of regulars who enjoyed a good story and a cocktail or *six*. And of course the Faust Club with it's raunchy burlesque shows. Only God knew when he would return and that's when the agony would begin, the worrisome ruminations, the *litany* Mother uttered unendingly.

"What's going to happen? Where is he? Where is the car? What is he doing? When will he be home? What if someone sees him? What if he loses his job?"

Unanswerable and unknowable questions, especially when asked of a helpless child. I could not answer nor could I reassure. Instead, I took on this worry. Unable to cope and without parental support, I'd retreat upstairs to my pretty room with the four poster bed, Empire dresser, chenille bedspread and flowered wallpaper where I would sit alone on my bed and just shake and shake while vigilantly waiting for the taxi to arrive bearing my sometimes lovely but now *stinking, falling down* father. I remember feeling as though there was no floor in my house, no *terra firma,* so unstable was my existence.

Life in my house was focused on my father's weekly binges and the gut wrenching rage, emotional abuse, fear, loneliness and sometimes his crying jags. The crying made me feel unsafe and the fear and worry made me feel terribly insecure. I needed my father to be strong for me. At the very least I wanted to be able to count on my mother for support. I needed *someone* to take care of me. I felt as if I were drowning.

'Finally,' I would think, 'Here he comes. The taxi driver is helping him out of the car. He's so drunk he can't even get the money out of his pocket to pay the cab driver.'

'Why? Why does he do this? It's always the same thing, falling up the front steps and into the front door. Are the neighbors watching? This is so embarrassing. . . '

'I'm not going down there, even if he screams.'

Calling up the stairs, he would bellow, "Get down here! Where are you? You ungrateful. . . . I'm home, God damn it. Get down here!"

From the top of the stairs, I would beg him to stop. "Stop yelling at me," I'd plead. "You're drunk—drunk again. Why do you do this?"

For a long time as a child, I thought I had some power over him. I still believed he would stop drinking if he really loved me. . .

I'd plead; "You're drunk, drunk again. Why do you do this?" I couldn't figure out how to stop him. Nothing worked. I thought, 'Maybe if I'm nicer or what if I'm meaner? Would that work? If he would just stop then we could be a normal family.'

He was ruining everything.

On and on it went. If I went downstairs, and most of the time I couldn't stop myself from going, the yelling would continue until he'd have something to eat and finally pass out.

Daddy was an angry, resentful, blaming, falling-down drunk. At some point along the line I learned from my mother how pointless it was to confront him when he was like this. So, his tirade would continue. Sometimes I'd just stay upstairs and wait it out or Mother and I would busy our selves elsewhere in the house, while Mother muttered:

"Hopefully he will pass out soon and sleep it off."

'How could I ever have a friend over with all of this going on?'

"You make me drink. It's your fault." He'd bellow at me.

Where was my mother in all of this? Mostly trying to avoid my father and the trap I'd learn to step into. I'd shudder with repulsion while cleaning up the stinking mess; the ashtrays full of cigarettes, Scotch, beer, food plates and spilled stuff until everything looked relatively normal again except of course for the imposition of once again, the *elephant in the room*. So there he was asleep, smack dab in the middle of *our* living room. Asleep and quiet for now while we engaged in damage control; doing things like, finding his car.

Once awake, my Mother would begrudgingly cook a big steak and baked potato to help in the sobering up process. That's when the *bitterness* would set in. We hated him like this. We were furious. Our silent scorn, our chilled "hello" upon his awakening, this hell we were living in, the feelings of entrapment were continuous. We looked forward to sanity breaks when Daddy traveled abroad for work. Those were the peaceful times.

Even though I didn't normally enjoy being at home alone with my mother, we seemed to manage pretty well when Daddy travelled. It was less stress for sure and gave us a little time together, to regroup. It was during those times together without Daddy that we really had time to reflect on what we were going through and what we might do to make things better, for us.

The strangest thing, most nights when Daddy was away, my mother would ask me if I'd like to come sleep with her in her bedroom. I'd say yes but really I didn't want to. I'd get into bed next to her, turn off the light and then after settling in bed, she'd reach for my my hand. The first time she did it, I was horrified. She never had time for a hug and whenever it did happen, it was like hugging stone. Her long thin fingers always felt like ice.

Always.

While he was away we'd talk about divorce or I did anyway. I wanted them to divorce but she would have none of it.

"Women, she said, just don't divorce their husbands. We make a commitment and stick it out."

"But, what about me? He won't stop drinking and yelling at me, I can't stand it."

She nodded. She understood, but she murmured, "I

can't, I just can't."

Her attitude infuriated me. The one person who could stop this intolerable situation just couldn't or wouldn't take the steps needed to do so. I felt so uncared for. This was the thing; I wanted her protection and I could see I was never going to get it.

I began to hate the weakness I saw in my mother. My disdain for weak and powerless women was firmly set in place. And as angry as I was with my father I began to yearn for his power. He seemed to get away with murder while my mother remained the hapless victim. I wanted control. I hated the vulnerability of women and I was not going to one of them.

Daddy's business, selling and exporting large earthmoving equipment, took him all over the world to North Africa, South Africa, India, Saudi Arabia, Thailand and other developing countries, often for months at a time where he was free to do whatever he wanted without interference.

Much later Mother told me he had a secret life while away, meaning mistresses and call girls. I know he enjoyed the famous opium dens in Bangkok where international businessmen would be served by exotic Thai women. He went there regularly when in Thailand but much later he said he dared not go back, so great was the opium high.

My good looking, well spoken, well dressed father, at his best, was a perfect host, great at entertaining clients and they loved him. When sober, he was absolutely charming and always had a good story to tell. He knew the best places to take clients all over the world. Daddy was really, really fun, until he wasn't.

When back in the States with us, he was either drinking, not drinking, overeating or on a diet. Moods and attitudes changed with all of these. Drinking gave him license to eat anything, drink anything, stay out as long as he wanted, stumble, fall and be as mean as he could be.

One day in the mid-fifties, while my father was at home after a four day bender, two men arrived at the house. Mother said they were from AA and here to help him stop drinking. How weird that these two men would even know about my dad's drinking. Wasn't this supposed to have been a well guarded secret. I was both shocked and hopeful. What were they going to do with him? Take him away? Fix him? Expose him? Was the jig up? I hoped so. This situation, this life was hell. Would he ever stop? Would I ever get out of there? Daddy told them he didn't want to stop drinking and certainly didn't need their help, even though they said they had a solution.

Not long after the men from AA stopped by, when I

was almost ten; I heard a public service announcement for Alcoholic Anonymous, Al-Anon and Ala-teen on the radio. My ears perked when the announcer said there was a meeting in the area for children and teens whose parents were alcoholics. I thought, 'maybe Daddy won't go to AA but I could go to Ala-teen.' This could be the life preserver I so desperately needed. I wanted so much to talk with other kids who had the same problems as me. Until I'd heard that service announcement, it had never occurred to me that other children might have some of the same problems I had. I thought I was the only one.

Later that afternoon, before my Father came home from work, I nervously and excitedly asked my mother,

"I heard on the radio today that there is a meeting for kids who have a parent who is an alcoholic. It's downtown, on Fridays at 5:30. I *really* want to go. May I?"

Pausing briefly and with exactly no enthusiasm in her voice, she said, "Well, how would you get there?"

"Would you take me?" I asked.

"I don't think so", she said. No, you can take the bus."

'The bus,' I thought. 'I'm 10 years old for God's sake and the meeting is at night. Forget about that.'

I can't tell you just how trapped and completely alone and unloved I felt at that moment. I have always regretted not being able to go to those meetings. Even at that early age I understood her reasoning; going to that meeting could expose the alcoholism in our family and that was a risk she wasn't going to take even if it meant denying her child the chance to begin healing.

It was at this point I realized I was going to have to take care of myself without the support of my mother. I could no longer stand this hell. I couldn't tell anyone what was going on.

"What happens in this house stays in this house."

Not a word much less a tear was to be shed on the outside. The thought of anyone knowing about all of this was embarrassing in and of itself. The problem with no one knowing was it kept me all alone. The shame of his drinking overwhelmed me. My mother's anxious fears made me feel unsafe, and my father's emotional abuse—the screaming, blaming, and curt remarks—hurt me to the core. Pretending none of this was happening was just crazy. Yet, I did it for many years. Oh, how I prayed for it all to stop. Miraculously at age ten I did get some really good news. Mother told me I would be going away to boarding school at fourteen for my first year of high school.

Some children might have been crushed at being told they were going to be sent away to boarding school. Not me.

For this young child in an alcoholic family, this news was just the life preserver I needed. I was thrilled. I did wonder why they were sending me, what their reasoning was:

'Was I too difficult?' Probably.

'Had my mother finally had it with me?' Very likely.

'Was she trying to spare me from the problems at home?' Maybe.

Finally, I would be out of there. Hope, I finally had something to look forward to even if it was an excruciatingly long four years away. Seeing the out I so desperately needed, I immediately said,

"Why wait till I'm fourteen. Send me now I begged."

"No," they said, "Not now." I'd have to wait.

Eventually I would be free.

I knew I was supposed to love and worship my mother but I didn't. Beyond that I was *furious* with her. She made no effort to protect me. I didn't get what I needed and I didn't need what I got. I didn't need the chilly facade, the superior attitude, the famous terse, stern grimace indicating her vast disappointment in me. I didn't need the *poor Mommy, Daddy's drunk again scenario* while I was the child left behind. Ah yes, and of course '*Poor, Poor Me,*' I guess. But that's really the way it was. I didn't yet understand how significantly hurt my mother was or how much pain she must have been in.

Things never improved for me as a child. It was impossible to have friends from school and if I'd had any I wouldn't have been able to invite them to my house. All hope had been abandoned for any kind of positive change. Daddy wouldn't accept help and Mother refused to allow me to get any. At a standstill, I waited four years in limbo for my saving grace, boarding school.

So, when did my *Mommy* turn in *Mother*? I'd been wrestling with this for weeks. I didn't feel close to my cold and superior mother and every time I said "Mommy" I just cringed. It felt *wrong*, dishonest. I'd try to be gentle.

"Mommy, I'm older now and I'm thinking I shouldn't be calling you Mommy anymore."

I later heard her speaking to my father. "I don't know, she just said she was going to start calling me Mother."

Mother felt right. I never called her Mommy again and I never told her the real reason. I spared her.

School friends were hard to come by. . . but the neighborhood kids were my closest friends. Most days we'd hang out at their houses or outside, mostly down in the woods by the ravine or the reservoir close by. We'd run around like wild children, enjoying our freedom. When the street lights came on, it was time to head home.

My friend,Michelle, a French girl had the *nicest* mom, Marie, a Corsican woman who loved to talk about France while making fantastic French food for us. She'd play the piano and chat endlessly. I spent many afternoons after school with Michelle and Marie in the safety of their home. I, of course never talked about the insanity at my house.

My other neighborhood friend was Portia. Portia's mom was the 1950's, hyper-organized, perfect wife and mom. She'd have the weekly plan written on a chalkboard in her kitchen—everything from Portia and her brother, Mike's school activities to what they were having for dinner each night. It felt so nurturing to me. I thought it was so cool. Mrs. Dinkins had it all under control.

Mother and I had heard Mrs. Dinkins was in the midst of writing her first novel but little did we know our family would be a big part of the unfolding drama. It seems Mrs. Dinkins had given a rough draft to Marie, hoping for a critique and a bit of editing. Apparently Mrs. Dinkins' novel was all about our little neighborhood. She included a story about a well known affair between two next door neighbors, Mrs. Leonard, a tennis pro and Mr. Abbot, a local CEO.

She wrote another chapter about a reclusive divorcee who seemed to be getting stranger and stranger and more harsh portraits of others in our neighborhood. A good bit of the book was devoted to *our* family, *my* father's drinking, and as if that wasn't bad enough, she continued on with less than flattering tales of my dear mother and the neglect of her only child. . . me.

You see, Mother did manage to have a life outside our house. Mother was well known as a big time volunteer. She was on the board of the YWCA, the Vestry at her Episcopal Church, a Red Cross volunteer, and belonged to the American Association of University Women. The truth about my mother is that she had a hell of a hard life. What seemed like smooth, proper, outer life was actually, as I have diagnosed here, delusional grandiosity, sharply juxtaposed with a lonely, hidden life of secrecy and pain. *Not that I have an opinion on all of this or anything.* Apparently Mrs. Dinkins had opinions of her own.

In the book, Mrs. Dinkins said, that if my mother were to be nominated for Coronation Lady in Peoria (an award for Volunteer of the Year,) she would have to inform them that while Mother was doing all of this amazing volunteer work, her own child was often being neglected, left with neighbors, baby sitters, her drunk husband or all alone. Marie was horrified but thought it in Mother's best interest to tell her. Mother was, of course, shocked, hurt, angry and defensive. "How could anyone think such things?"

Later however, when I was almost twenty, she told me everything about the book. Mother never told Daddy. She wanted to share with me a very painful part of her own story. What her telling did for me was *amazing.* I wasn't horrified. I knew it was true. I was gloriously validated. It had been confirmed. Things *were* bad in my house, I *was* neglected.

I began to sense early on that the ways you could live and be that Mother approved of were extremely limited. The dilemma started with the Italians. I went to school with some Italian kids. I liked them so much. They had what I wanted... big families, involved parents and fun parties with grandmas, grandpas and cousins. Someone was always cooking up meatballs in sauce, sausage and peppers. The adults were drinking wine while the kids were having a blast running around. These kids were fun and so were their parents. Their families did things with the families of other kids in our school. I envied that. I had been to one of their parties and afterward I went home and excitedly told my mother how nice the kids were and how they had *great big fun* families.

I asked, "You know the Greco family? They had the best party. They have five kids in my school. They're so nice. Do you like them?"

"I know who they are. They are pleasant enough."

"Pleasant, so you like them?" I asked.

"They're okay. But you know they're not cultured."

Not understanding, I said, "Cultured? What does that mean?"

"It means speaking well, having good breeding, being well read, knowing the arts."

This concept was foreign to me. I thought we were supposed to like people based on whether they were *good people*, nice, fun. . . not these other things. And how on earth would I be able to distinguish the cultured from the uncultured? This was *the most confusing* idea to me. So, for several years I would point out someone who I thought was ok, nice, someone *I liked* and I'd ask,

"Are they cultured?"

The German family a block away, no, 'not cultured.' It turns out Germans were *no good*.

The Dominican nun, no good, she was Italian from the South Side of Chicago.

Anyone I tried to be friends with, *no good*. One day I said to my mother. "So the Italians are not cultured, right? But they *are* popular and they seem to be *happy*. If we are so *cultured* and so great then why are we so *unhappy* and *miserable*?"

She had no answer.

So there it was, even if you were a happy, nice person,

loved your family, were involved in school activities, ran a business, you could be almost 100% sure not to measure up to my mother's standards.

So if everyone was rejected except according to Mother, the cultured, and if the Mid-Westerners rejected everyone whom was even a tiny bit different. Then who *was* ok?

I discovered there were all kinds of categories that could make you unacceptable, and very few guaranteeing acceptability.

I gave up. I gave up trying to figure it out. I gave up trying to please. I couldn't please my mother and my family was too different to please the status quo. I would reject these stringent norms of acceptability coming from both my family and my community. They were stifling the life out of me. This was a huge turning point. Although the culture concept had become deeply ingrained in me as my own judgment tool, I consciously try to reject it to the best of my ability. It was then I decided if *no one* was any good and I liked them anyway, then I wanted to be with those people, the ones who didn't measure up, the fun ones and more than that, the *interesting,* perhaps even the bizarre ones. I would become one of those people myself. Mother thought no one else was *good enough* or *acceptable* and she was miserable. She chose to remain with her often drunk and emotionally abusive husband. She chose *not* to rescue her child from a painful situation. I saw her as *weak* and *powerless*. I would not be as powerless as she so I staged a healthy rebellion and began to explore *all* the things she found unacceptable. The great irony was by training me to live a "proper, cultured and acceptable life," my mother killed any desire in me to be like her, to accept what she found acceptable. The narrow parameters she lived in—or at least thought and pretended she did—felt to me like *iron bars*. Not only were these prejudices crushing the life out of me but they were mostly a façade. Although we had come from a couple of proper family trees, there was no fooling anyone; things had gone terribly awry in our branch. We presented a front of acceptability but the truth about us was sad, very sad.

The day was fast approaching when I would leave my family and I would *not* turn back.

Chapter 3

AS A SMALL CHILD I already had an eating issue. As a baby I would cry for *BaBa* -bread and butter. I refused to eat anything else. Why would I, BaBa was *so* good.

Food issues still loomed large in my house. My mother's fear of food and being overweight began to further mar our relationship. Mother had fought with me about *my* eating since I was almost five. She had been a middleweight most of her life and seemed to enjoy eating but suddenly she was highly disgusted by larger portions and took enormous pride at having strict control over food and the ability to eat *very* little. Maybe having two overeaters in the house was getting to her or maybe food was the one thing in her life she *could* control.

My love affair with food started early on, around the time I stole candy for the first time from the funky luncheonette near my house—the one with the pink and gray, boomerang patterned Formica countertops. My best friend Kathy and I would casually saunter in just to say *"hello"* to the owner who kept a small bowl of Hershey's Kisses on the counter for his customers. We'd chat him up a bit while *sneaking* the candy into our pockets, right in front of him and he never said a word.

Along with food binging I was learning to use various *illicit* ways to get what I wanted.

One Saturday morning, Kathy and I were given quarters to buy kites at the local 5&10, right next door to the luncheonette. We'd gotten quarters in the morning and somehow both lost them almost immediately. 'How could this have happened?' We wanted those kites so badly we could *taste* them. Now what? We were prepared to do almost anything to get them.

Great idea, we'd walk in there and we'd just *take* them. We'd been getting away with taking the candy, hadn't we? Kathy and I finalized our plan during our six block walk.

The kites were all the way in the back of the store just beyond the cheap china, beyond the candy bins, the housewares and shampoos. There they were, in an umbrella stand container. Standing tall were the kites of many colors. Kathy chose red and I chose blue.

The coast was clear. . . one behind the other, we walked out of the store with the kites held tightly against our sides, straight up against our legs. Feeling very sure of ourselves, we stuffed handfuls of candy in our pockets from the candy bin on our way out the door.

Once safely around the corner we quickly ran home to have fun with the kites.

The next morning, while sick in bed with a cold I heard the phone ring. Mother answered.

"Hello. . . Yes. . . Really? I see. . . I am so sorry. . . I'll get back to you."

"*Oh no.*' I thought. Somehow I knew, as soon as she answered, who it was on the phone. My face flushed from embarrassment as she confronted me.

"That was the man from the 5 & 10. He said you and Kathy took the kites from his store yesterday. What happened to the quarter we gave you?"

"I know. You gave me the quarter and then I lost it. When Kathy realized she lost her money too, we couldn't believe it and decided to steal the kites. I know it was wrong. I'm sorry."

"I'm sure you are sorry but you will have to pay the man back and go in there and apologize."

We went back and forth on, "Do I have to," and "Yes you need to own up to this."

I agreed.

Embarrassed and at my mother's insistence, the next day I found myself back at the scene of the crime, humbly apologizing for stealing the kite, even admitting I'd stole the candy too.

I truly *was* sorry, but the embarrassment was even more unbearable. She was right to make me confess, to learn about repercussions of my actions. *Tough lesson. . .* That was the thing about my parents, even with all the chaos, they always made me own my own behavior, fess up and apologize. It was a one way street that way.

Kathy Hernin was my best friend from first grade till third grade. She laughed like me. She ate like me. She seemed to be just like me. I didn't know what was going on at *her* house and if her parents were alcoholics or not but when I'd go over there I'd see at least thirty beer bottles on living room tables, (*but who was counting?*) and always a big mess in the kitchen. The beds were never made and the sheets were never changed. It felt creepy to spend the night there—*those sheets.* She was my one friend in grade school that I could relate to and we had a lot of fun together even if it was mainly felonious.

Her father was a local TV sportscaster who was eventually transferred to California. I couldn't believe that they were leaving. I couldn't believe I was losing my friend. I was beginning to understand the impermanence of things, of everything.

It was 1956 and I was I was about ten when Mother started working as a family social worker for the City of Peoria. This was completely ironic since her *own* family was such a disaster. She kept a record of her daily lunch expenses in the tiniest spiral notebook I'd ever seen, jotting down with pride just how little she spent on herself for lunch at work each day. There were entries like: Oct.6, lunch 75 cents.

She was getting thinner and thinner. She'd brag, "I had been a size fourteen for a long time, then a twelve and that felt so good I decided to go to a ten and just like that, now I'm an eight."

She was far *too* thin. Watching her lunch on Melba toast, apple slices and a couple of nuts made me crazy. Forcing herself to all but vanish was one thing, but she continued to turn her critical eye to me. She was always on me about my weight and I must admit, I was overweight and a super sneaky binge eater.

By 1958, everyone and your mom had discovered mother's little helpers, amphetamines. Chubby little pre-teens were routinely prescribed diet pills and I was one of them. Mother thought, 'this little pill would do the trick,' and I would finally be an acceptable weight. She had thus far been unsuccessful in controlling my eating and my weight, nothing short of drugging me would do.

In truth *I* wanted to be thinner. How great it would be if this magic pill could make me beautiful and popular. Would these pills help me lose weight? Maybe I'd finally get my mother off my back.

How else would my world change?

My issues with food were far more complex than merely needing to curb my appetite. I wanted to lose weight and be more attractive, but I had been sneaking food at home and binging on my way home from school for so long, this wouldn't be easy. Food was not only my delight; it had become my *secret* pleasure. I even began to revel in the *illicit* means I used to get it, the loose quarters, dimes and nickels I'd find in my mother's purse or my father's sock drawer. It didn't take much...doughnuts were only a nickel and, being frugal, I usually took advantage of the special; three for 12 cents. There were the doughnuts, chips and ice cream I'd devour on my way home from school, before I'd be forced to consume dinner at home, so I took it upon myself to fill up beforehand on what satisfied me, sweets.

When Mother took me on our drug seeking visit to my pediatrician, I had lots of questions for Dr. Leigh.

"What is this pill? Will I be thin? How much can I eat? Will I lose weight? How much?" I was hoping for a *magic pill*, the one that would make me lose weight without eating any less. The nurse asked me to step on the dreaded scale. At 12 I'd hit a 120 pounds. I was mortified. Dr. Leigh jotted something in his notes. What was he writing? He explained I should follow a diet plan and suggested that drinking a glass of water before each meal would fill me up and make me less hungry. I thought, "Oh yea, sure, that'll work."

After we paid our bill I looked at the office visit summary. Dr. Leigh had written on his form, 'obese,' in the weight slot, then crossed it out and replaced obese with the word 'overweight.' I felt so ashamed. I was obese? I must be close to it. He had changed his mind, *not obese,* just overweight. I thought obese people were huge.

'Was I really huge?' I had no idea—I had learned a couple of other behaviors that day—rationalization and denial. I told myself, *'Thank God I'm not obese.'*

I'd gotten my prescription for some green and white diet pills. 'One a day for thirty days,' it said. A new adventure would begin. At the time not much was known about amphetamines. They weren't considered an addictive drug at the time, but they made me jittery, nervous and *ridiculously irritable* which played havoc with the already tenuous relationship with my high strung mother. Before the pills, we argued constantly, now we were having screaming matches.

On the flip side, I liked the appetite curbing effect and the speed demon, crazed, whirlwind energy amphetamines gave me. I felt on top of the world. I was a complete self-contained package who filled every moment with the utmost determination. If anyone interrupted me, however, I would be so agitated I'd want to scream. So thus began my life on an emotional swing. My moods would vary according to how exhilarated or not my high would be. Sometimes I'd have to eat just to calm down. This was a self-defeating proposition at best. I didn't see the speed trap I'd stepped into.

Meanwhile, a few years earlier, I had honed a perfectly drugless way to numb out while in grade school, to completely space out, by daydreaming. I could transport myself to foreign lands, create a new family or be off having a blast somewhere and totally be *there* and not in class, except for my body which still occupied a seat in the classroom. And yet, I couldn't understand why every report card said, 'doesn't concentrate.'

Escape was becoming my goal. But now I'd found new ways to numbingly de-focus. There was Dramamine and *its* effects. My parents and I drove to Florida every winter for a several week stay. I adored the beach front apartment we took in Belleair Beach on Florida's west coast. It was great to get out of the long Midwest winter, but the thought of driving to Florida with my parents was intolerable.

Since I was car sick on most of our trips, my parents gave me Dramamine to quell the nausea. I soon discovered another effect of the drug. Taking these little pills put me out for a few hours. *Perfect.* I loved this. Zoning out was great. I eventually became the keeper of the Dramamine and began to self-medicate every four hours or so. Never wanting to miss lunch or dinner, however, I'd ask, "Please, wake me for meals." In my exploration in *how to live* amidst turmoil, I had found a life preserver of sorts, a way to get to Florida and avoid having to interact with my parents.

So by the time I was twelve, these escape routes were my journey to the land of *Out of It*: food, Dramamine, spacing out, and amphetamines. And I was Out of It. *Anesthetized.* I began to realize if I didn't like the way I felt, I could change it pretty rapidly with just a pill or a little *mind vacation.* I stopped using Dramamine after my childhood. I didn't like the hangover I got from it and by that time I had left home and ceased having family vacations.

Amphetamines would accompany me for the next twenty years. I wasn't a big user. I didn't like the inconsistent edge they provided. I'd be up and on top of it one day and crabby as hell the next. I was a very small but fairly consistent drug consumer. In my adolescence and later in my adult years, my friends, who would qualify as heavy users would laugh at me. For their every four, five or more pills I'd take one or even a half. They called me *The Nibbler.*

The bottom line on all of this was, *I didn't know how to be, how to live,* and *react to life and to others.* With no parental examples or siblings to bounce things off, I was lost and confused much of the time. What was normal? What *was* the right way to be?

As I write about this early part of my life I get clearer and clearer on this journey. The steps of my journey were laid out in my early childhood. Journeys take you somewhere. I never imagined where this one would take me.

Chapter 4

MY EIGHTH GRADE CLASS was having gradu-
ation complete with caps, gowns and a school dance. It felt
like a formality, just like the rest of my life. This was the
culmination of all the waiting and all the praying. For years
I'd had one secret desire, escape. I needed a real and total
escape from my surroundings and graduating eighth grade
was an important stepping stone on my journey out of Peoria
and on to a new adventure. My hope was to never see anyone
from my school or ever go back to Peoria again.

I would be off to boarding school in the fall, *if* I passed
the entrance exam for the Convent of the Sacred Heart in
Lake Forest, Illinois.

Unlike Peoria, the town of Lake Forest was amazing. Beautiful houses lined every street and the attractive town center had everything I could want or need. There were great stores, a good burger joint and a park. I'd studied the colorful brochure daily for months, imagining myself in my uniform, walking down the heavily wood paneled halls to classes, just like the girls in the brochure. I pictured myself in the former nuns' cells, now used for boarding school students. The tiny alcoves seemed so small, just big enough for a single bed and a tiny dresser. Yet this would be my hideaway from the life I wanted to get away from at home.

Here I would be free for the next four years *if* I passed the entrance exam. How could I possibly pass? I'd never paid one bit of attention in school. I'd done okay, but having day-dreamed and drugged my way through it, I feared I knew *nothing*. I couldn't *possibly* measure up. All this was racing through my mind during the Dramamine free car ride to Lake Forest.

As I reached the study hall where the test was to be administered, I was *stunned* by how many students were there. There must have been seventy-five perfectly preppy girls, all looking test ready with #2 pencils in hand and then there was. . . *moi*. I thought, 'Oh my God, how will I ever measure up to these girls?' There I was, experiencing my first *anxiety attack.* My hands were shaking, I couldn't breathe. I was a mess. I'd never felt this way before, so much depended on my passing this test. Fitting in with these girls would come later, I hoped.

Much later, I would realize the deep source of my panic.

My grade school dream and prayer was always to fit in. Actually it was to be popular. To go from having lived a life of avoidance and escape and being basically friendless and backward to popular would indeed be a stretch. The thing I'd carried with me from Peoria to the study hall full of very prepared-looking girls was this: I didn't know how to make friends outside of my neighborhood. To me, popularity meant being in control. The popular girls had it made, I thought. Everyone wanted to be with them, do whatever it was that they were doing. Popularity and control were the things I craved as much as I craved food, drugs and escape. My life had been out of control for *so* long because I had been so *seriously* controlled, in ways of which I was only vaguely aware. It wasn't just the emotional abuse I was running from, it wasn't just the alcoholism or the control over my food and it wasn't just the neglect, coldness and superiority of my arrogant mother.

It was *so much more.*

So many children have had more horrific things happen

to them. I wasn't raped, no attempted murder and there was no *purposeful* ritualized abuse. Yet I have a fear that what I am about to recall, which lays at the root of much of my deep anxiety, will ruin the image people close to me have of my parents. The truth is, however, their experiences and memories do not tell the full truth which emerges in incidents like these, from which I so badly wanted to escape.

Rough treatment. My mother insisted upon bathing me with a rough, line dried washcloth. She would scrub me so roughly up and down my arms and my legs. Eventually after my appendages were sufficiently sterile, she would wash my back. Then, rough and seemingly with great determination she would scrub and scrub *my* private area.

"Ouch, ouch, stop, please stop," I would beg.

"I have to get you clean."

And she continued, scrubbing me so hard. It was not just the roughness that hurt so much, but her determination while she was doing it. So many feelings came up for me each bath time. I felt dirty. At least my mother thought I was. Why was she so rough with me, so disinterested in my pain?

The question begs to be answered. 'What was she thinking? Why, when I asked her to stop, wouldn't she? Why so hard and so determined?' She would bathe me in this rough manner till I was eight years old, clearly old enough to bathe myself. Eventually I had a come to Jesus, battle with her.

Screaming, I said, "I'm done. I can take my own baths. You hurt me. I don't need you to bathe me. I can do it myself." These bathing sessions had made me furious. I created such a screaming fuss that she had no choice but to stop.

Although I had not been entered I had been invaded and violated. Had I been the brunt of some kind of sexual anxiety on her part? Or had her cleanliness obsession made her completely insane?

As I write, I find I am *red hot* angry. This is how I felt as a child. I was so angry with her. I can feel it now. Although I have forgiven her, the memory brings the feelings up raw and fresh. It's very real. It's a heart-pounding anger, and I want so much to run and escape from her, not physically, but from the emotional mark she left on me while scrubbing at my body.

The body invasion did not stop there. I had another rather strange sort of problem with her. It still baffles me today how my mother, although neglectful for the most part had a flip side that was really inappropriately invasive. She was absolutely obsessed with whether or not I'd had a bowel movement.

There was never a day when my mother didn't ask me, "Souvenir, have you had your BM today?"

Mother would say this anywhere; in the house, out of the house, in the supermarket, out on the street, in front of friends, anywhere and as loud as can be. I'd beg her to stop, but she wouldn't. I couldn't get over her behavior, how she embarrassed not only me but herself with such strange rantings. I was so embarrassed and the shame of it lingers still.

I knew that it was irrational to bathe me the way she did and for so long. I knew intrinsically, it wasn't her business what went on in my body or came out of it. My body was functioning perfectly well without rough treatment or constant prodding. This invasion of my person made me feel powerless and anxious.

I don't believe my mother was intentionally trying to hurt me. It was something else, perhaps something buried in her own history. But I knew I had to get away from her.

Then there was my father. He could be great when sober. But the drink changed him, brought out demons and made him say things he never would have said had he been sober. Some of the things my father said would mark me deeply.

At fourteen, he wanted me to start wearing little high heels, a lipstick and some cute red, heart earrings. Some girls might have loved the idea, but wearing these things was absolutely *not* what I wanted to do. All I could think of was—*I'm not ready. I'm not ready.* I felt pushed into it. I realized there was something about me that my father wanted to change. He kept insisting. I flatly refused. I tried on the heels and I couldn't walk in them but he kept pressing.

"What's wrong with you? Why can't you walk in heels?" Once again I felt invaded, judged and shamed.

That same year, I'd begun to shop in the boys' department for things like big comfortable sweatshirts. One day Mother confronted me with a worried look.

"Why do you like to wear boys clothes?" I didn't know really but I sensed a palpable fear in her voice.

"They are just oversized sweatshirts. I like them because they are big and comfortable and *so* soft. . . and they fit me."

Shortly after, she asked, "Have you read *The Well of Loneliness*? It's a well-known lesbian novel written in the 1930s."

"No, I haven't."

"There is a copy in the living room."

I was confused. Were my parents afraid there was something "off" with me, just because I wanted to wear loose-fitting sweatshirts? Were they trying to cut me off at the pass before I made it to the finish line and came out as a lesbian? Or was the suggestion that I read *The Well of Loneliness* an invitation to see that I wasn't alone in the lesbian feelings she suspected? And I had questions when I found the book in the living room. It was an old, dog eared paperback. She must have had it for a long time. Why did she have it and for how long? I read it and was jolted by how it made me feel. It brought to the surface feelings I had never felt before.

Adding even more to the confusion and sense of invasion, Daddy would talk about my breasts. "How did your breasts get so *big*? No one in our family has big breasts like that. Have you been playing with them? Is that why they're so big?"

How the hell did I know how my breasts got to be so large. It sure wasn't because I'd played with them. At fourteen, I wasn't even certain what he meant by that.

I didn't know how to reply. This felt like an accusation. My breasts just grew out of my body the same way my arms or teeth did, naturally, without any help from me. How could playing with my breasts make them grow? What was he saying? Had he implied I was weird and not like the rest of the women in our family, breast-wise? The invasive comments continued.

Daddy said. "I like the feel of a woman's breasts on my back."

Why on earth was he telling me these things? I was hurt and confused. I wasn't sexually mature but still I had a vague and disgusting uneasiness that my father had provocatively and inappropriately brought *my* breasts into his fantasy world.

These are some of the powerful influences driving the panic attack I fought so hard to control the day I had to face the Sacred Heart entrance exam. I didn't just want to get in, I *had* to get in. I had to escape my *own* home.

The day I learned I'd passed the exam brought huge relief. I'd be leaving my parents and shed the constraints of Peoria, Illinois forever. I'd have a new life that *I alone* would control. I promised myself that I would *never* let anyone or anything take control away from me. I'd wear what I wanted. I'd go where I wanted and I'd do what I wanted.

Chapter 5

THANK YOU GOD.

I was accepted into the very Hallowed Halls of the Convent of the Sacred Heart. When the news arrived, I can't tell you how relieved I was. I could barely sleep. This would change everything. I would leave all of it behind, my parents, my neighborhood, my school and Peoria. Now, I thought, I would have a chance to live a normal life, get away from my family and from *everyone's* dysfunction, except of course, my own.

Now I had work to do. The rest of the summer was spent preparing myself, erasing even the remotest inkling that I had spent my entire former life as what I knew was an awkward, unattractive, overweight, confused, desperately unhappy child.

The quest for perfection had begun and there was so much that needed to change. Problem—nothing fit except extra large size clothes. I was still big—around 150 lbs and I had become *so* self-conscious about it, weighing myself every day—while still compulsively overeating. I had to lose weight before I left for school in the fall. I didn't want to be the "fat girl" in school, so I put myself on the "Speed and Campbell's Soup Diet." Desperate to lose, the next month I ate nothing but soup and coffee, downed with Eskatrol, the time released amphetamine I'd been taking since I was twelve. These pills hadn't worked so well to this point, but on my new "diet" I fairly rapidly lost twenty five pounds.

So far, so good—what else did I need to do to fit in? A list emerged of things I wanted to change. Needing help with certain things, I approached Mother one evening while she was making one of her low-cal specialties, chicken a la king made with skim milk for dinner. Disgusting, right?

She turned from the chopping board. "Are you getting packed for school? We are driving you up to Lake Forest in three weeks."

"I am, but I'm thinking I might need your help. I want to start my new school *fresh*—get my hair frosted and some new clothes, glasses and some other things. Can I? Will you help me?"

"OK, make me a list and I'll take a look at it."

Kindly, she sprang for what I'd asked for. Then Mother came up with the idea of having my hair streaked at the local beauty school, where the salon workers were beauticians in training.

"I want lots of really light streaks with dark showing through, no yellow, please." I told the student in training.

For the next hour, the trainee pulled *every strand* through the painfully tight-fitting rubber cap.

"Not so much. Are you sure you're not pulling too much through?" I asked.

"No, it's fine."

But I was thinking, 'What the hell, stop it you idiot.' I knew he was doing it all wrong, I just had no clue how to stop him. He gave it a good rinse, removed the cap and *presto* I was a yellowy, orange, horrified redhead.

Too shy to say anything, I bolted out the door and ran directly to Bergner's Department Store, bought myself a box of Ashe Blond hair color, hoping no one would see me. Problem solved. Not so bad. I was, I thought, finally Sacred Heart acceptable. I would fit in and I would be dazzling.

We ordered the plaid uniform skirt, blazer, gym uniform, two white shirts and the required navy and white Spalding oxfords.

It dawned on me that probably way more than my hair, weight and clothing would need to be changed if I really wanted to fit in and I *needed* to fit in. I knew I wasn't *enough* or even *likeable*. I was willing to change myself into whatever I thought was acceptable.

In grade school I paid close attention to the most popular girl in school. I wondered.

'What is it about her that makes her so likeable other than the fact that she's so pretty? Whatever it was I would mimic. I could walk like her, talk like her but I could never *be her* or be like her. "But, what is it that makes a person popular?" I asked an older girl in my neighborhood.

"Being nice and being friendly." She said.

Being nice? Being friendly? Really? I'd thought of it as more of a skill, a skill of manipulating people to like you so you could be in control. That's how clueless I was going in my first year of prep school. So, not having great people skills, I could look good on the outside, I could have nice hair, I could even be thin, but would these things make me cool? Happy? Win friends? Would I finally be ok?

Daddy drove Mother and me up to school and as excited I was, I was also a *wreck*. Other boarding students were arriving at the same time. There were quick, excited welcoming "hellos" and brief introductions. Dads carried the big stuff while the moms and kids lugged the smaller items up the two flights of the grand staircase. Older students guided us to our small cubicles and lockers.

The moment arrived when we parted. "Are you all set?" my father asked, smiling.

"Give us a call soon. Sensing my apprehension, he said, "You'll be ok. I love you."

It was weird. Even with all the things that had happened I knew he loved me.

"Good bye dear, I love you too," Mother added.

I knew she did on some level but still I felt so unlovable.

There were sixty of us boarding students. Checking everyone out at dinner that evening, I couldn't help but wonder. Who were these girls? What were they doing here at Sacred Heart? Why were *they* sent to *this* school? And always I worried about me, me, and me? What were they *thinking* of me?'

My first few months, in fact, were spent figuring out this boarding school thing. I so desperately wanted to be liked so I smiled *all* the time to appear *friendly*.

Then one day, one of the nuns came up to me in study hall and said, "Stop your constant smiling. You look like a Cheshire Cat."

Embarrassed at first but then I thought, 'Good point.' I *knew* I was overdoing it.

Mistakes, I made lots of mistakes—trying too hard, people pleasing and not keeping confidences. I talked too much or not enough. It wasn't easy, this trying to fit in.

As I got to know some of the boarding students I realized some were from less than model families as well. How would a kid who was this awkward find her new crowd?

The feeling of being an outsider did not leave me. When I was in what seemed like *normal* homes I felt the old sense that I was the "odd girl out," and when I stayed in the homes of girls whose families had *issues*, I felt like we were both "odd girls out." Would I ever shake this outside-looking-in feeling, a sort of 'them against us' comradery had begun to form. The rebel inside me was at that moment born.

Sallie's alcoholic mother physically abused her when drinking and she had the scars to prove it. Ricky had some sort family dysfunction and her grandfather had been a part of the Chicago Mafia. Mary's father was mentally unstable. There were more, I'd heard stories but I didn't pry. I was learning not to ask too many questions.

And then there was *me* and *my story*, which hovered around me even there in the safety of boarding school. There were questions I managed to dodge. I just couldn't reveal myself, even when others spoke about their family's problems. I was trapped in some combination of too ashamed and too loyal to talk about my family. After all this was a new start for me and I *liked* the idea of leaving all of it behind, while adhering strongly to the, "Don't tell anyone what is going on in this house rule."

These new friends were great and like me, they weren't perfect. I was starting to put this friendship thing together, find girls who had issues, like I did. My wanting to be popular began to fade. Just having friends was enough.

Most of the students at the school were from 'upper-class' Irish Catholic families. The day students lived in the suburbs the North Shore of Chicago in Lake Forest, Wilmette and Winnetka and most had gone to school together before coming to Sacred Heart and were already friends. But they were open to making new friends and a fun, welcoming bunch. I got to know some and spent lots of weekends at their homes or at the homes of the other boarders.

I didn't know then that the answer lay in this: I was carrying secrets. All that mattered was that I maintain them and there was so much I needed to hide.

Mother had a rule. I was to only come home from school on Thanksgiving, Christmas and Easter. Not only was I very hurt by her decision but this was also a *huge* embarrassment for me. Most of the other borders went home regularly or their parents visited. In fact, their parents *begged* them to come home every chance they got. Even though I was happy at school and didn't really want to go home much, this created a *huge* contrast between the other girls and me. They were wanted. I was wanted only once in a great while. The sting of rejection hurt so badly and only further confirmed a feeling I'd carried much of life, I really wasn't wanted. The bitter truth was that my parents didn't want me around.

Not surprisingly, I found the need to be rebellious and was often in trouble with the nuns. I loved the *power* of stirring up a little drama. One weekend I instigated a little prank by coaxing the weekend borders to hide for an afternoon at a remote end of the building, just to torture the nuns. I knew they'd panic, thinking we had escaped. What fun. When we were found after a few hours, they *were* furious.

I relished being away and feeling safe from the wildly changing emotional landscape at home. In fact, I hoped I would find a *home* here at school, perhaps even warm feelings and a sense of being nurtured. The nuns were so smart and like the Jesuit priests, they were well educated, broad minded, scholarly and even fun sometimes and I liked that. But unfortunately I didn't find them as a whole to be nurturing. Maybe if I hadn't been so *defensive* and emotionally *awkward,* they might have been more so. If I had a connection with *any* adult I might have felt more grounded, settled down and better behaved.

As a result of my shenanigans I was often called into Mother Connor's office to discuss my behavior. I wasn't keeping my cubicle up to standard, I talked in the hall and I was sometimes late. These were not "horrible things" but *substandard* nevertheless.

Something was driving me. I had a desire to get out of this box. My old, old issues, were returning in a new form. Boundaries were for other people, boring people, people who had found their place in the world. I hadn't.

The inner drive *to get out of and to escape from* something was getting stronger. My friend Mary and I decided to exit campus one afternoon. We left through a break in the fence and this was forbidden. Wasn't a big deal for us. We did it just to get to the other side, go for a walk and hang out on some swings on the property just beyond campus. One of the older nuns saw us sneaking back and wrote us up. The ruling: a two-week suspension. Mother was absolutely *furious.* I couldn't tell if she were angrier about the *reason* for the suspension or because the punishment was for *two weeks at home with her.*

And then there were natural curiosities driving all of us adolescent girls. One of our greatest curiosities at the school involved the nuns themselves. Exactly what went on in the nun's quarters? Were they sleeping together? Were there couples? Or was that just a fable? Did they drink? How long was their hair? What the hell was going on in the convent?

Of course we had no access to the nun's quarters, but our laundry room was next door to their locked, double door entrance. We'd try to steal a quick peek into the small windows at the top of the doors, but saw *nothing*. There were rumors of raids on their quarters by former students while the nuns were away, but we had no clue to their findings. For us, glimpses into their private world came only in stolen moments. . . and by accident.

One day a group of us were outside on the weekend playing soft ball. Our happy and really fun, youngest nun Mother O'Hara was in charge. Mother O'Hara was standing at second base while I was at bat. Strike one, strike two and I hit the ball far left field. I ran for first base then on to second. As I arrived at second, I suddenly realized Mother O'Hara had just then knelt down to tie her shoelaces. As she began to rise I ran on to the tail of her head-piece, pulling the entire ensemble off of her head and leaving her standing there, revealing blond wavy hair and the face of an embarrassed, pretty young woman. Clutching her garment, she *ran* for the closest available door. We now knew. Inside that habit contraption lived a *girl* like us.

"Mother, I'm so sorry," I said later.

"Yes dear, I know."

By the second year I finally had friends. My social ineptness had started to fade and I began to fit in. I was so excited and grateful that this struggle of mine was beginning to turn around. My parents still allowed me home just for the holidays, so my weekend visits to the homes of friends continued.

One night my friend Patty and I were in twin beds in her upstairs bedroom. We'd had a great day, going to a football game and out with friends later.

Unable to sleep, I was shocked when *overwhelmingly strong* feelings swept over me and a *desire* for my friend. This was something new. Out of *nowhere* I wanted to be close to Patty, to be in bed with her and embrace her. My feelings were so intense. I was completely surprised and shocked. My sexual feelings for women had just *at that moment. . .* emerged.

Before, I had been curious about other women's bodies, but never aroused. What was I supposed to do with this unbelievable feeling? I was trained to suppress my feelings, *all of them.*

I knew the rules:

Don't feel.

Don't talk about anything.

Never admit.

Always deny.

This inner boundary was very strong. Added to it was the tremendous pressure I felt to be socially acceptable. This was something that had been drummed into me from the beginning. And now this pressure to do something I knew was unacceptable was going against that. It was as if two tectonic plates were grinding against one another somewhere deep within my being.

I felt overwhelmed by a shame *so deep* I might *never* swim out of it.

I didn't know what to do with this new feeling.

One voice inside me said, 'If I'm having these feelings then maybe it's in the air. If I'm feeling it then maybe she is, too. After all, she seems to like me.'

The other voice said, 'What if she doesn't feel the way you're feeling.'

I didn't know and if I did know I wouldn't have acted on it.

I thought, 'it's a one time thing.' I chose to ignore it. But something had changed.

When I was back in Peoria for Christmas, I had begun to notice a couple of women about town, mostly at the grocery store. One was feminine-looking and attractive, while the other looked—*different*. She had thick glasses and a sort of back woods look, unattractive really. She wore flannel shirts, sported a short bob hair-do and always wore jeans.

I was fascinated by them. Always together, they seemed to take care of each other. I would study them whenever I saw them. I'm not sure how I found out, but someone told me they were *lesbians*. Later on I found out where the local gay bar was in Peoria. I didn't drive yet but whenever my parents and I would drive past there, I would hope I'd see my subjects going inside. I never got any further with this but they were secretly my great curiosity.

Soon enough, my four years at boarding school were coming to an end. College Boards were taken and my scores were okay.

My parents arrived on graduation day, as expected. Mother in her turquoise, ultrasuede suit and heals was in full drama mode, tearfully wringing her hands.

I was confused. "What's wrong?"

"Are you graduating?" she asked.

"What? Of course I'm graduating. It's graduation day, that's why you're here."

Daddy rolled his eyes and interrupted. "Mothers' worried when you go up to receive your diploma they'll make an announcement that you're not qualified to graduate and won't get your diploma."

On this day, *my* graduation day, a day that was supposed to be full of joy, felt ruined. My heart sank, I was crushed. Didn't she have any faith in me at all? Did she really think I wouldn't graduate? My grades were average, but not failing. I couldn't believe she thought the school would embarrass us in this way.

Nonetheless, Mother continued crying. The tears flowed out of fear that she would be embarrassed by me, her daughter, who seemed to fail her in *so many ways*.

When the ceremony was over and I was saying goodbye to friends, I realized how much I hated leaving the safety of this place and how I was not looking forward to going back home, not even for a small part of the summer.

I'd dated a bit. I'd felt safe enough to feel my sexual feelings, but not free enough to explore them. I got to spend great times with friends. I did what I set out to do, and had been given the grace to have a place to do it. Sacred Heart nuns were known for instilling empowerment in their girls and I began to feel like I could do anything. But what *was* in *store* for me.

Exiting boarding school was a very different experience from leaving grade school; no longer did I feel like running and leaving everything behind. I was beginning to miss my friends and the school, just at the thought of leaving. Was I ready to move on? I didn't know but I was willing.

Mother allowed me to apply to only *one* college. It was her cheapness and not understanding the need to apply to several schools that informed her decision. She *infuriated* me. What if I didn't get in to the one school that I had applied. I knew this was unrealistic and after some unsuccessfully begging I had no choice but to go along with her on this. So now what?

Wanting to go out west for school, to get even farther from my parents, I applied to Colorado College and big surprise, I didn't get in. After the rejection and panic had set in and passed, I applied to a college placement service and was accepted by twelve schools, making me feel like less of an idiot. Most were nice, women only schools but my parents insisted I choose a co-ed school because, *you know,* fear that I might not eventually find a boyfriend. I picked one of the few listed, Ottawa University in Ottawa Kansas of all places.

Meanwhile I would spend a couple of months before going off to college at the Ranch in Lake George, a Dude ranch, where had I worked for a few years with my cousins in the summers. We bunked together in funky cottages just up the trail from the man lodge. This was a fantastic place for all of us. The Ranch, as we called it had over six hundred acres of beautiful pasture land; riding trails, woods, several pools, tennis courts, lodging, dining rooms and bars. My Uncle Joe started the business in the early Fifties.

The bar scene was enormous, with popular bands playing every weekend in the main lodge. My cousins and I loved hanging out at the huge bar and dancing. I was just eighteen, the New York State drinking age back then, but my cousins and I had been drinking at the bars in town since we were sixteen. At sixteen, the drinking thing was new to me but I aced it. Having larceny in my bones, I had cleverly changed my driver's license from born in 1946 to 1944 by horizontally and thinly lifting and switching numbers with a razor blade, making me legal or look like it anyway.

Lake George was a fun tourist town with shops, restaurants, tons of bars and of course it's gorgeous lake. During the day we worked at the Ranch, enjoyed the lake whenever possible on our days off but at night the bars beckoned. With absolutely no supervision we were free to do what we wanted as long as our misbehavior wasn't obvious. The family didn't want to know and we didn't mention it either, a sort of 'don't ask, don't tell.' We'd quietly sneak back to our bunkhouses in the wee hours, hoping to avoid George, our oldest cousin, the Ranch manager.

My cousins, from my father's Irish side, a close bunch, lived the rest of the year in the Albany suburbs and summered in Lake George and often travelled as a pack. They are a good group and I love them. It was so great being a part of the family. We all liked to go out to the bars. It was there I got to enjoy bar hopping myself.

One of my cousins, Jay, is gay and has known it forever. He and I would take off for a bar on Rt 9 called Mr. Chips before hitting the straight bars. This Adirondack version of a Gay Bar, a lot country and a little bit rock n roll, not a drag queen in site, had lots of draft beer and flannel shirts. I'd never been to a gay bar before coming to Lake George. The site of two men or two women dancing or kissing for the first time was bizarre to me. I knew about being gay in theory but I was just beginning to see a little bit of gay reality.

We'd later join the rest of the gang at the Station, a popular grungy bar with cheap beer, good bands and a fun vibe. It was a hangout for college kids and I couldn't get enough of it. We'd dance and hang till closing time, then sneak back to our bunks.

Life was always good at the Ranch.

After getting back from spending the summer in Lake George, I had one month to get myself ready for college. Back on my soup diet, I got blue tinted contact lenses and some new clothes. I had no idea what this new school would be like. Everything about the Kansas school seemed weird to me. It was a Baptist school for one thing. I had no clue what *that* would bring. I'd managed to find my way around the hallowed halls of the Sacred Heart' so I was pretty sure I could adjust to this new school as well.

I hoped.

Chapter 6

MY JOURNEY to Ottawa, Kansas was a *trip* alright. The afternoon westbound train left Chicago's Union Station right on time. On the train by myself, with too many bags, I settled into an empty group of four seats, giving me plenty of room for my things and to take a nap. Joining me on this excursion there must have been over a hundred college kids. It was party-city on that train and over the next couple of hours a group of us had formed a pack, meeting up in the parlor car pretty late in the evening for a drink.

After the bar closed, we headed back for more. I watched as some of the boys violently broke into the beer cases. This was hard to believe, I'd never been around such blatant disregard for someone else's property. I thought, 'should I

leave and go back to my seat? What if a conductor shows up?'
But no one did. That's when the real party began. Feeling
somewhat innocent, after all, I rationalized, 'I'm not the one
ripping into the beer cases.' but I was *absolutely willing* to
drink the beer.

Back at my seat after taking a nap and just a little
hung over, my thoughts turned toward this new journey
of mine. I was headed to Kansas of all places. 'God, what
was I thinking? What was in store for me now on this new
adventure?' I'd always had goals for myself. What were they
now? Other than finding a boyfriend and leaving my family for a new kind of independence not many goals came to
mind.

My uncomfortable feelings about men had dissipated
for the most part. I dated a few of the local fellows at home
the summer before college and honestly they were *not* great
experiences. After the prerequisite chat, movie or a bite to eat
they were always ready to pounce and very insistent about
it. I didn't like the presumption that I should be ready for
action or having to defend myself if I wasn't.

What kind of guy did interest me anyway? Well, certainly not someone I'd have to push off me on the first date.
I wanted to have some fun, get to really know someone, let
it build and then. . .

I didn't know exactly what I was looking for back in Peoria but what *did* interest once I got to school in Kansas was the rumor that fifteen guys from the East Coast had just arrived at the college and were sharing a house off campus. The idea haunted me so one afternoon I took myself over there. A bunch of them were hanging out on their front porch; a good looking, nice looking crew, Jim, Tad, Andrew and Jake.

It was the curly haired Jim who interested me. After some time together, I could see he was a little rebellious, like me. He was irreverent like me and hysterically funny. Meeting Jim was to change my life forever. I hadn't known what I was looking for but I knew it when I saw it.

Now I had it all, a boyfriend, a friend, a buddy and what felt like *family*. And he liked me right back. We were drawn to each other from the moment we met. I fell for him immediately. I was completely taken with him.

Jim was from Philadelphia, very cute with an *irresistible* teddy bear quality. Never had I met a guy like him. There was none of the nervousness I'd had before. I'd never felt comfortable dating before, something about it scared me. Boys terrified me and I just wasn't comfortable around them. But I was completely at ease with him. Inseparable from the start, we were like glue. I loved his warmth and his sweetness and when we kissed, I couldn't believe it. He kissed me. I hadn't felt this way before and when he held me, I felt loved and safe.

We spent most of our time together, walking around town, meeting the characters, stopping in at the local bars. Later we'd go to the funky doughnut shop near his dorm. We'd hang out till midnight when the best, freshly glazed, hot doughnuts were ready for sale. Yum. It wasn't till a little later that we would discover the local bar scene.

We both hated the college rules. They seemed silly and we comisserated constantly with each other. It was 1964 after all and rules like, no jeans, no smoking, and no drinking in the housing off campus, seemed extreme. Ottawa was essentially a dry town; the only inebriant allowed to be sold or served was very low alcohol 3.2 beer. The rules and the low content didn't stop us from enjoying a couple of the local dives. Despite the 3.2 beer, we just drank more and all day on the weekends—pitcher after pitcher at these places.

Jim and I met some pretty interesting characters in those spots, like the local bootlegger. Miss Miller who made booze runs to Kansas City to pick up and then deliver to some of the dry counties. Bootleggers were from the south I thought and made their own booze, but not here, Miss Miller was just your run of the mill booze runner.

Miss Miller's daughter, Marta, was the local call girl. Never did I ever think I'd spend time with a call girl and I could only imagine what my mother would have thought, but I was pretty sure Daddy would have been amused. Marta became our bar friend, hanging out with us in the evenings until she got a call on the bar phone and off she would go. At only twenty, I wondered how she got into the business. She and her mom had cornered the market on a couple of rackets in Ottawa.

On one run, Miss Miller picked up a bottle of Scotch for Jim. It was this bottle that got him in a lot of trouble. He and a couple of the guys sat around having drinks one afternoon in Jim's room. They asked Mark, a local guy who was also living at the house to join them. Demonstrating a *complete* lack of appreciation for the hospitality, Mark reported the drinking episode to the school council. We didn't know it but Mark was a part of the *God Squad* who reported various infractions.

Jim was soon asked to leave the school. We were horrified at the injustice, but on the other hand, didn't he know the risk? I couldn't believe he was so careless. He left, I stayed, but got on the first train back to Peoria after the rest of the semester. Ottawa University wasn't a good choice for me either and I felt completely lost without him.

My relationship with Jim was far from over. We weren't going to let a mere expulsion get in the way of our relationship. Soon enough I found a new school, Harcum College in Bryn Mawr on the Philadelphia Main Line, not far from where Jim lived. I had developed an interest in fashion by this time and Harcum offered studies in business, fashion and textiles. Perfect.

By late August, Jim and I would finally be together again after not seeing each other for months. The anticipation of our new life starting in September was so exciting. His parents had invited me to spend a week with them until it was time to settle in at school, giving us time together.

Jim helped me get settled in my dorm suite with its large double rooms connected by a bathroom. My three roomies seemed like nice girls, also with boyfriends. They, like me, spent every moment they could outside the school with their friends.

The students were primarily Jewish girls from the New York area and looking for an "MRS degree." Most were engaged with enormous engagement rings by their second year and married soon after, very traditional.

For us, nothing had changed and yet everything had changed. We were still the same kids we were when we met in Kansas but now the circumstances and the scene had changed.

As traditional as these girls seemed to be, they had something that I admired. They seemed to know what they wanted at such a young age. They had a plan. Some of them were looking at houses with their fiancés. Control, they had control and a plan. They had a willing partner who was on the same page. This started to look good to me. On the other hand my "not wanting to be conventional" side was winning.

Seeing Jim in his suburban Philadelphia setting opened my eyes and I realized, as it was turning out, he was much more of a *wild boy* than I had suspected. Just like me, Jim had been prescribed amphetamines in his adolescence but he liked them a lot more than I did, *a lot more*. Neither of us used them while in Kansas, but here in suburban Philadelphia he carried a small vial with him most of the time and took them much more frequently than I realized.

In his own natural habitat, Jim was a different animal from the teddy bear I'd met in Kansas. He had his amphetamine prescriptions, but when the demand exceeded the legal dose he found unscrupulous doctors who filled the need. I went with him sometimes to a doctor in North Philadelphia.

I was taken aback, not relating to the strung out motley looking crew of skinny people lined up out the door, waiting for an audience with this Dr. Feelgood. A one stop shop, he was known for handing out large quantities of black beauties. First he'd write the prescription and then fill it. Coming home with one hundred twenty at a time seemed like a lot to me, but they quickly disappeared. I had been an *as prescribed* user but Jim was using many more than I had previously suspected. His consumption didn't alarm me at first. I hadn't yet made the connection between *his* consumption and *his* behavior.

It wasn't long before I met my new best friend at Harcum, Suzi Gold, a beautifully zaftig, hippie chick with the best long, dark, frizzy ringlets and natural blonde streaks. She had the kind of hair most girls would want to bend, straighten and blow into submission but not Suzi. With a Sophia Loren face and sweet little joint-rolling hippie fingers, to me, she was the coolest thing.

I made friends with Suzi, because she was *not* a princess yet still a *beautiful* girl and sweet but possessing a bit of a dark side. Suzi, with her poison rings, flowery tops, threadbare bell bottoms and silk scarves was a patchouli-scented, free spirit. We were quite the pair. She *was* a free spirit. . . but totally neurotic. She worried about everything, yet in my eyes she was free because she *acted free* in spite of her fears.

We were physical opposites. I was the tall, fair-haired Mod, Twiggy styled Mid-western, slightly chubby girl to her dark Sofia and the attraction was electric. Amazingly spontaneous, my patchouli, sari and jean-wearing Suzi set this blonde paleface free in more ways than one. Locking her suite doors and unlocking my passion, while the roomies were away gave us the moments we needed to free ourselves with each other. We two were home.

I wasn't looking for this. I hadn't thought of loving a woman for awhile. But this was no fantasy. She was as real as it gets and so was I. The only issue was Jim. I felt I needed to tell him about Suzi. He knew I'd questioned my sexuality. We'd told each other everything up to this point, so I'd felt safe being open with him.

"OK," he said, as long as I'm still number one."

"Yes. You definitely are."

Then I knew I had room for both Jim and Suzi in my life. Maybe not Suzi for the long-haul, but being with her let me know I could be with a woman and I could also be with a man. I wanted that man to be Jim.

Suzi, this free bird, loved her pot and her dope-dealing hippie boyfriend, Mark, on Long Island near Roslyn, where her parents lived. Mark sold more than pot and, I think, acid.

Suzi liked acid, but not me. I wouldn't dare take the chance of losing control.

One fall afternoon Jim and Suzi and I were hanging out in Jim's car in front of my dorm at Harcum. I made sure the subject of drugs came up. Suzi had joints with her, and I wanted to try some. She shared a joint with us, our first. No reaction at first but not being *quitters*, we bought an ounce and then another... and another....

Pretty soon we were smoking *all the time*. We bought from Suzi and smoked until there was no more. My goal became to smoke until almost unconscious, fading in and out of reality. If I was looking for a way to escape social boundaries I'd found it with Suzi. Funny, but I'd never smoked pot at Sacred Heart or even in Kansas. But this wasn't Kansas anymore, was it?

Not surprisingly, I don't remember most of my second year at Harcum but some things became indelible, including some things I would have been more than happy to forget like being invited to a Holiday party at Jim's high school friend's incredibly beautiful home, where I was encouraged to drink, a lot. Everyone kept saying, "You're no fun. Drink, drink." Swayed, I drank way more than my comfort level. Here was the thing: Before we'd left Jim's house for the party, we'd filled a large commercial coffee urn full of "you name it" whiskey sours, made with every kind of booze you could find in Jim's parents' cabinet and a minimal amount of assorted juices. At the party I quickly downed four or five of tumblers of whatever they were shoving at me. That was more than I'd *ever* drunk, and suddenly the room began to spin. In minutes I was so drunk I could barely walk. I needed help to the bathroom and proceeded to throw up all over their pristine, gorgeous bathroom for the remainder of the party. I tried to clean it up but there weren't enough towels, so I stuck my head out the door and screamed for more, "Please." Jim helped me finish up and took me upstairs to the master bedroom on top of the guest's coats. I was a *horrible* mess.

This was not my style. I hated being out of control. But the fact is. . . there I was. . . totally out of control. Was this what I needed to get totally out of my old self? Now I'd had an unfortunate episode with alcohol. Not good. It would be some time before I realized, this was not exactly the path I was looking for as a way out of the person I thought I needed to escape, which was me.

My favorite friend of Jim's at the time was Bill. I was looking for a voice of reason and I found one in my new friend. Such a nice guy, and he was in keeping with the kind of people I knew at Sacred Heart. Bill was a student at the Philadelphia College of Art and came from a big, Irish family. Jim and I would often go to parties at Joe's art school buddies' apartments. I loved the scene. They were smart, Bohemian, artsy and informing me with a new philosophy. I was eager to take it all in and grow. Joe was always there for me when things got out of hand. And they did. When we partied, we would sometimes have to take Jim to the ER. Doing too much was becoming a regular thing.

As for me, a real interest and appreciation for art, fashion and the bohemian was forming. I loved eccentrics, artists and characters. I fancied myself as some kind of social anthropologist, finding out about people, who they were, what made them tick, and reveering them for their eccentricities.

Rapidly, I was integrating myself into a bizarre new world that lay beyond the bounds of the so-called "normal," everyday lifestyle. Now, being different took on a *positive* spin, more sure than ever that I would not associate myself with the mundane, nor would I be ordinary.

Sometimes Jim and I would take off for New Hope, Pennsylvania, for the day or the weekend. New Hope was an old-school artist colony. It was actually the home of the art movement called the New Hope School of Impressionists, located in a historic, beautiful town full of the eccentricities I now craved. It was a great escape to the freedom we craved.

New Hope was a hippie haven in the Sixties, Bohemian, funky and artsy. When going to New Hope, I dressed in wild caftans and lots of beads, while Jim let his curly hair go into an Afro, wore Indian-print shirts and bell bottoms. We'd get high and parade ourselves around New Hope like the rest of the crowd. We were fascinated by the hippies, the artists, the art, the café and bar scene. New Hope had an unofficial open door policy for all and still does.

When at school, Suzi and I talked about poetry, writing and the City Lights Bookstore in San Francisco, the hippies there, Dylan and Ferlinghetti, Timothy Leary, Ram Dass and tripping. We were anti-establishment. We hated commercialism, the unfairness of almost everything, suits and *The Man*.

Because of the times and the consciousness-raising talks with Suzi, I came to see that there was more to life than just me and my personal issues. There was a big, important world outside *my* tiny, little world. There were world concerns. The outside world was in the midst of turmoil and change. I became concerned about these things and they too became a part of me. I began to embrace some of these issues into my life. I wrote poetry and studied the writings of the Beat generation.

Still, drugs were a big part of the scene. Getting high was a huge, even though Ram Dass said, "Be Here Now," we were anything but. We were only too eager to get out of our heads and just *out of it.*

Other boundaries were coming down too.

No one worried about what had been the big terrifying no-no for previous generations of unmarried women (and men, too, I suppose), which was, "getting pregnant," "out of wedlock." At least you weren't worried if you had birth control pills. As soon as I was sexually active, I ran to Planned Parenthood for my first supply. We were now free to have sex without the worry of getting pregnant. Not just me but our entire generation.

By 1970, we had been through so much politically. There was the Vietnam War, with our soldiers dying, so many of us in protest and resisting the draft. On the brink of nuclear annihilation, we endured the Bay of Pigs. President Kennedy had the families of America building bomb shelters, while the children of America were hiding under their desks. We had the Cuban Missile Crisis, and the horror of our young President being assassinated and then his brother Bobby, and our Black American Gandhi—Martin Luther King Jr. who was shot at the Lorraine Motel in Memphis, Tennessee.

My generation was angry. We were angry in protest and in our hearts, but we preached love. We were the LOVE generation. Love and protesting were the answer. But all the tie-dye, all the pretty flowers, all the marching, all the protest and even Woodstock could not put America back together again. John Lennon wanted us to imagine, but The Stones knew we weren't getting no satisfaction, Ferlinghetti and his staccato words telling stories I couldn't tell but needed to hear. We had Greenwich Village and coffee houses. We had Bob Dylan and meaning in our words. *We* were anti-establishment. We wanted change.

Of all, Ferlinghetti and Dylan spoke to me the most. These edited passages from *I Am Waiting* spoke to me, because this jaded child was indeed waiting for a rebirth of wonder, on so many levels.

I Am Waiting
By Lawrence Ferlinghetti

> I am waiting for my case to come up
> and I am waiting
> for a rebirth of wonder
> and I am waiting for someone
> to really discover America
> and wail
> and I am waiting
> for the discovery
> of a new symbolic western frontier

and I am waiting
for the American Eagle
to really spread its wings
and straighten up and fly right
and I am waiting
for the Age of Anxiety
to drop dead
and I am waiting
for the war to be fought
which will make the world safe
for anarchy
and I am waiting
for the final withering away
of all governments
and I am perpetually awaiting
a rebirth of wonder

I am waiting
to get some intimations
of immortality
by recollecting my early childhood
and I am waiting
for the green mornings to come again
youth's dumb green fields come back again
and I am waiting
for some strains of unpremeditated art
to shake my typewriter
and I am waiting to write
the great indelible poem
and I am waiting

for the last long careless rapture
and I am perpetually waiting
for the fleeing lovers on the Grecian Urn
to catch each other up at last
and embrace
and I am awaiting
for a new rebirth of wonder

Thinking back on these times and these ideas—I would

later write:

18-22
while Dylan
prophesied
the Village
steamed a new beat
in summer
Joni got sad
as
parking lots
erased
the pretty trees
and
hairy Beatle bugs
landed
on
the
Ed Sullivan Show

Stones
souls rocked
like
a Black church on dope
like I like
and
Panthers fists raised in
mad cat rage
our
President
was
shot
dead
while I was busy
just
trying
to
be
a person

It was 1967, college life was about to come to an end, I was twenty one and graduation was almost upon us. Toward the end of my second year, Jim proposed or was it that we just knew we would marry. It was a given.

At this point Jim was doing the bookkeeping at the famous jeweler J. E. Caldwell in Philadelphia. He bought me an amazing engagement ring and just like that, we were engaged. We were to have a small wedding at Saint Joseph's Catholic Church in Cheltenham, Pennsylvania. This was the same church with, the same priest, Father Gallagher, who had tried to bless the Faraco house years before, only to be thrown out by Jim's mom.

"My house is clean enough." She told the Father Gallagher.

He knew the family well so when it came time for our Catholic marriage preparation classes; Father pulled me aside and gave me a stern warning: "I hope you know what *kind* of family you're marrying into." I didn't ask and I didn't want to know. I'd take my chances.

So, I was getting married, a new adventure, a new life for which I might or might not be prepared. Even though our wedding was to be small there was still a lot of planning to do. Suzi would be my maid of honor, actually my only attendant. She and I chose a beautiful three-quarter-length, pale pink, chiffon dress which looked amazing on her.

Then there was *my* dress. I wanted something different, *of course*, not a typical wedding dress. So, loving fashion I designed my own dress with the help of a dressmaker. It was a three-quarter length, A-line dress in white silk, with a pearl and crystal, two-inch border around the stand up collar and at the cuff of the three-quarter sleeve dress.

Invitations were designed and sent. We invited mostly immediate family members and friends to the Barclay Hotel in Philadelphia for a luncheon reception. Jim's mom had sent invitations for everyone to come back to their house for an early supper. She wanted to include local extended family members who weren't invited to the wedding.

With my dress, asymmetrical Sassoon haircut, Mikimoto pearls and antique pearl and diamond earrings, I was ready. Jim looked amazingly handsome in his dark suit, white shirt, tie and gold cufflinks.

So we were getting married, a new adventure and a new life. Reality was beginning to set in.

What was I getting myself into?

I know now our situation was sketchy at best. Jim and I took very little in our lives seriously. If I could look myself in the eye back then, as the adult I am today I would say,

"What the hell are you doing?"

Chapter 7

IT WAS JUNE 5TH, 1967. I was twenty one and Jim, twenty two on our wedding day. The weather was so incredibly beautiful. Our best, well laid plans were at last coming to fruition. The guests were in attendance, beautiful white daisies and yellow roses adorned the church. The gorgeous Barclay Hotel in Philadelphia was ready for our luncheon reception and an amazing feast by Jim's mom was prepared and waiting for later in the day. Life was good. Even Father Gallagher seemed to be all in and in a surprisingly good mood.

So we were to be married, a new adventure, and a new life but reality was setting in. I had crazy thoughts running through my head. Was this the right thing? We were *so* young. We loved each other but we weren't conventional in any sense.

'I can't imagine not marrying him. What if I'm making a huge mistake?'

I answered this question myself.

'I don't know but I'm going to take a chance.'

We flew to Miami Beach for our honeymoon enjoying the beach, the Follies at the Fontainebleau Hotel, Cuban restaurants, bar hopping and more than anything, after recovering from serious sun burns, each other. We were away from it all, free. . . but after a week, it was time to head back to our little apartment in Philly and to our jobs.

I had just started working at the preppy Ladybug store on Chestnut Street while Jim worked with his dad and brothers in their cutlery business. Highly determined to move and start our own business, we saved every penny we could for our eventual move to our favorite place, New Hope. One year later, and having no clue about what moving to New Hope might mean to us in the long run, we made our move. Renting an idyllic looking, super sweet, green shuttered, white clapboard, two bedroom house with a picket fence on New Hope's Main Street looked to us like the perfect setup for a couple of newlyweds. Something about this felt eerily familiar, reminding me of my first house in Peoria and all the hopes and dreams of my parents.

Every weekend, wildly clad tourists strolled in and out the many shops and restaurants on our part of Main Street, creating a colorful day time picture, but a more intriguing scene and the *real* action took place elsewhere and into the night. It would be awhile before we found these places for ourselves.

New Hope was a very different story on the weekdays, when writers, artists and shop owners would met for break-fast or lunch, gossip and chatter, at Mel's, the tiny, funky, bohemian, coffeehouse on Mechanic Street. New Hope had and still has its share of the exotic. Many of the more bizarre members of wealthy families found themselves attracted to the New Hope bohemian lifestyle. Janine Witte says in the book, *Embraceable You*;

"New Hope is the place where the "black sheep," from all families come to stay."

It was at Mel's where some of these fascinating minds would meet.

Now, I'm *not* an intellectual but I *am* a thinker. I loved soaking up the local tales, the history and new ways of thinking. I was after all, now in the land of Rodgers and Hammerstein and the summer home of the writers from the

Roundtable at the Algonquin in New York and just down the road from Dorothy Parker's house.

Jim and I, at twenty-two and twenty-three were the new kids in town and we didn't go unnoticed. The older set; doctors, lawyers, business owners, decorators, antique dealers, New York folks with weekend houses and of course Odette Myrtle and her gay-boy entourage, all noticed. We were the very fresh, young newcomers.

Odette was a wild, French, former Ziegfeld Girl, film star and owner of the well regarded French restaurant, *Odette's*, on the Delaware River in New Hope. In many ways she epitomized the wild and edgy spirit of New Hope, a spirit into which we were happily diving head first.

I had two passions, food and jewelry. I'd study them both whenever I could. Our good friend, Dee Rosenwald had studied at the Cordon Bleu in Paris, not long after Julia Child had been there. Dee, an amazing cook and an inspiring teacher, had wonderful exotic dinner parties at her house on the Delaware River. Later I would copy her recipes when hosting parties of our own.

Both of my internationally-traveled parents possessed a well-rounded knowledge of world cuisines, jewelry, and design. Daddy always brought us amazing pieces of jewelry from his travels. When I was fourteen, he gave me a gorgeous

Aquamarine ring from Brazil—Aquamarine, my birthstone. It surprised me that he knew the birthstone for Aries, my birth sign.

When he told me the stone came from inside the earth and from a mine, I was amazed.

'How could something so beautiful have grown over thousands of years underground, unnoticed until that first person made the discovery?' I asked.

I was hooked.

So those were the delicious nuggets I cherished and these precious gems are the lovely bits I still adore and have inherited from my parents. Expertise in both of these has served me well, both in pleasure and in my professions. My parents also greatly influenced my journey into the culinary arts. They both had a deep interest in International Cuisine.

Jim and I eventually got big time into the bar scene. We still partied with the art school crowd in Philly and, of course, with our new friends in town. But that's not all.

We were preparing to open our store in a tiny retail space on the very old and very charming Mechanic Street, calling it, Jane Livingston's Antique Jewelry. We were to have Georgian, Victorian, Art Deco, Art Nouveau, Italian gold, American Indian and good fashion jewelry.

We'd been to all the local auctions, flea markets and

small antique shops looking for inventory but came up short on the more expensive, rare pieces. Jim and I decided to take a chance and went to New York looking for jewelry for the store. Our first stop was to see Larry Ford, the famous jeweler who supplied Barbra Streisand with much of her famous Art Nouveau collection.

We called Larry, told him a little about our shop, what we were looking for, and asked for an appointment. He graciously said, "Sure, come in on Saturday." We were unsure of ourselves and, not wanting any of that to show, we did our best to appear confident, sophisticated, and informed. Shyly, we introduced ourselves.

Larry was like a God to us, a rock star in the jewelry world. The next thing we knew, we were in possession of tens of thousands of dollars worth of the most gorgeous Art Nouveau, Art Deco and Georgian Jewelry that Larry had given us on consignment.

That's when I learned—it's okay to ask, because they might say, yes. So many people were very kind to us in New York on our inventory search. It wasn't as tough as we had imagined. Now with our newly acquired pieces from Larry, the store was ready to impress.

The excitement of opening our shop was an amazing experience. Sales were so good the first year that we were able to move to a nicer, larger space. Our friends stopped in to see us at the shop in the evenings, often to buy something and go out to the bars with us later. A favorite was the Canal House, a well known cabaret, across the street from the store. A favorite that summer was cabaret singer, Cynthia, who entertained us all with her funky renditions of things like Leaving on a Jet Plane, Suzanne and Norwegian Wood before we'd go to the Prelude to dance.

Rumors, there were plenty of rumors going around New Hope that Jim and I were drug dealers. For the life of me, I couldn't understand why. We got speed and pot in Philly and sold it sometimes to our friends—*at no profit of course*. Basically, you *could* get drugs from us sometimes. . .

Super cute and only eighteen, Michael Dwyer was my first New Hope gay-boy pal. Michael's deal was, he loved to create a scene just for the fun of it and believe me, every time he wore his unbelievably short, ripped up, cut-off jeans, a scene would be created. Nothing was left to the imagination.

I met Michael one day while having lunch at Mel's and he fascinated me. Michael was a cute, fun and mischievous troublemaker and trickster. Shock value ruled, anything for a reaction. We soon became the best of friends.

Jim was less than enthusiastic about Michael. He didn't love coming home after work to find Michael smoking our pot and having eaten everything in the refrigerator.

A few years later, Michael bought the revered Mel's with his partner Bernard, a Frenchman and called his new restaurant The Apple, where I worked occasionally.

Michael was fun but incorrigible. I'd be waiting on tables and he'd rush over to me like he was my long lost lover, grab me and throw me to the floor, jumping on me with howls of laughter, while all I could do was scream,

"Get off me."

There was no stopping him; I'd struggle to stand up. It was madness, *the poor customers*. It was always something like that with Michael. He is the same friend who only months later, at a dinner party, offered Jim a hit of speed, which of course he took. Turned out it was *acid*. Now that was a *big* surprise.

The barge party. It was our very first important social occasion in New Hope and we had been invited to a really *swell* barge party on the Delaware Canal. Again I was encouraged to drink more than I should have. I was always more of a long, slow and into the night alcohol consumer, but on this night I downed the drinks and then a really embarrassing thing happened. Mid-party and fairly inebriated, I asked the barge operator to dock the barge for a moment so I could go to the embankment to pee. Rather than heading for a dark area of the towpath where no one could see me, I made the inebriated decision to squat and pee in front of everyone. Uproarious laughter ensued.

Embarrassed and feeling dizzy, I stood up, hiked up my underpants and immediately fell backward and down the embankment, rolling head over heels through the ferns, weeds and the wet, rust colored, fall leaves, landing down at the muddy rivers edge.

The partiers howled as the old caterer, Bill, helped me up and back onto the barge. I'd had quite a tumble. My previously lovely, cream-colored dress was suddenly seriously camouflaged. Sick as a dog, I hung my head over the barge railing, puking all the way home.

Jim was having issues of his own that night. Reaching over to save an older man from falling down, he slipped and hit his head on the metal railing, completely splitting his ear in half. Grateful to get off the boat alive; we stumbled home and off to the hospital for stitches. We were quite a sight at the hospital; me in my grass stained dress and Jim with his bloody ear. None of the late night hospital staff were pleased, nor was the emergency room doc who had to be called in from home.

The booze had done a pretty good job of numbing Jim's ear, so not surprisingly, no anesthesia was required.

The next day and for some time, we were the talk of the town and not in a *good* way. We figured we'd ruined our chances for any social life at all, but soon enough, all was forgiven and we prevailed.

This was the big magnetic pull, Jim and I were the new thing, and we were invited everywhere. It wasn't just these more established folks who made up the social list. If you were fun, if you were amusing, if you were outrageous or famous, notorious for something or just plain beautiful, you were on the list.

Everyone drank and most of us smoked weed. Hell, if you were a dishwasher and gorgeous then you were in. This was the social set, a sort of café society. The women and the gay guys hit on Jim. The men and the dykes hit on me. The place was full of characters and we couldn't get enough.

Not long after moving to New Hope we met the two older queens who lived behind us on the river, Rob Scofill and Danny Abrams. Rob and Danny had been together for thirty years. With an escalation in their drinking over time, a certain attitude and deep lack of respect had set in. It had become a nightly ritual—drinks at Danny and Rob's. Every night they drank giant vodkas on the rocks until things got pretty nasty between them. Hurling insults at Danny, Rob couldn't get any meaner sending Danny up to his bedroom when he couldn't take it anymore. Time for our exit as well.

Eventually, months later, the time came for Rob to turn his anger on me. He had taken a liking to Jim. It wasn't reciprocal but the more he drank, the nastier he got, to me. At the time I didn't get it. I was still a wide-eyed, very innocent twenty two, just four years out of convent boarding school when this leg of my life began. We were babies really, so young to have thrust ourselves into scenes like this. I mean, hadn't I had enough of this sort of thing growing up?

Like many young people, I thought I knew it all. No one could tell me anything. If you told me that it might not have been a good idea to marry so young, or that we shouldn't be doing some of the things we were doing and hanging around with some of the folks with whom we were hanging around, I would never have listened. Not in a million years.

I had thrust myself into a world for which I was totally unprepared. New Hope was a wild place with people doing wild stuff, most of which I loved because I saw these things as a big *Fuck You* to the status quo but a lot of it scared me to death. Things like disloyalty, cheating and being cheated on, having multiple partners, doing outrageous amounts of drugs, personality changes and acid.—all of it frightened me.

All these interesting New Hope people, all of these choices were too much. We were all over the place, trying everything on, trying to fix ourselves with drinking, drugs, and sexual intrigue. There was a new morality and a revolution going on in society but in New Hope, these choices seemed to be boundaryless.

One evening Rob and Danny invited us for a drink, and to this day I have completely blocked the details. During the course of this get together, Rob verbally attacked me in a really hurtful way. I was crushed and meekly defended myself while Jim said nothing. When we got home I said something about how hurt I was and how surprised I was that he didn't defend me. Again he said nothing. I was devastated. I could see that something had dramatically changed in our relationship. It was like my life at that moment imploded. I felt betrayed and abandoned, the pain was gut wrenching.

Friends were to arrive a bit later for dinner at and not wanting to dampen the mood, I shoved the incident and the feelings in a tiny locked drawer somewhere very far away.

I mumbled to myself, 'I'm so angry. I need to work through this with Jim, find out what is going on here, to what extent things have changed.'

I knew that would take time and I didn't want to drag our friends into it. I knew for sure that they wouldn't comprehend this embarrassing situation I'd gotten myself into with Danny and Rob.

During dinner I wondered, 'what had just happened?'

Was I losing my husband? Was I about to be abandoned? Did he even care anymore? He didn't *seem* to care. His loyalties had changed; drinking and drugs ruled.

My early training was beginning to do me in. I had been trained from the start to be loyal. I had been trained to be in denial and to keep up appearances at all costs, at the parental school of denial. I was loyal to a fault. The loyalty I was taught to have was faulty in and of itself. It was a loyalty fostered by fear. . . loyalty undeserved, yet it was all I knew.

The scene, the drugs, the flattery, the temptation, our sudden popularity, this new moral code, fear and anxiety from living this way, pressure to make choices, all of these things were changing us. We were no longer the kids we used to be. I thought our exploration been anti-establishment out of rebellion but here was *more to it*. It turned out that *simple* rebellion had taken on a life and a power all of its own. Once I had been an excited and brave explorer. Now I was terrified.

Oh my God, I realized I had learned from the best. My denial, my illusions were *very* similar to my mothers. My perfect little clapboard house. . . now I knew what had felt so familiar. . . it looked perfect, just like my parents red brick house in Peoria.

'Oh no.'

I was a mess. I felt I was going to explode. . . and on this night I was terrified.

Something awful was about to happen.

Chapter 8

SO WHAT *was* this terribly frightening thing that happened during dinner?

After lots of "very serious weed," and copious amounts of red wine at dinner, we lingered at the table chatting. As I sat there, I started going in and out of focus *as usual* and laughing hysterically. Then I very suddenly blocked out, but not completely.

Then I spun *way, way off* into an absolutely frightening, black *nothingness*. I kept feeling myself falling in and then, down, being pulled into *deeper and deeper* depths, completely spinning out of control.

Then suddenly, I *was* back and then blackness, back, then blackness, again and again.

Total and complete panic set in. I came to, hearing myself screaming, "*Help. Help. Help me.*"

As I said it, even I knew my friends couldn't possibly have the power to pull me out of this terror. What would it take? I had gone into an uncontrollable, complete breakdown and panic mode. I begged for someone to bring me back to reality and away from this horrible state of mind. As I became more conscious I could see that my friends were laughing, thinking I was trying to be funny but Jim saw my struggle. Lifting me from the chair, he helped me find my way out to the porch, where I wretched for the next couple of hours. If only that had been the end of it, but it wasn't.

My heart beat wildly and uncontrollably as my mind raced and slowed, raced and slowed. Images of the blackness kept emerging, and with it, waves of terror. I was sure I was going crazy.

"Help."

On it went for days, no *months. . .*

Paranoia and severe anxiety continued to flood in at random moments. As for everyday living, I was completely dysfunctional. I had dry heaves, sometimes for hours at a time. Eating was impossible. I'd force myself eat a piece of dry bread a couple of times a day, just for sustenance. Everyday I either threw up or had dry heeves, my face broke into a new crop of gigantic hives. I wanted to go to the hospital, but I was afraid they'd keep me forever so I didn't. I was so panicked that conversation was almost impossible.

It seemed like there would be no end to this horrible downer and I had a relatively new business to run. The only saving grace was that it was January in New Hope, the slowest time of the year, which meant *no one* was coming into the shop. Everyday I'd go to the store and just sit there feeling as frozen inside as it was outside just waiting for this thing to end.

But on and on it went. I couldn't shake it and I needed help. I went to Farley's, the revered old bookstore in New Hope and bought every self-help book I could find on the subject of panic and anxiety disorders. I read them voraciously. Through these books I came to see that I wasn't alone in having panic attacks. My readings assured me the panic would be over when *I* decided it would be over. But on it went. I chose to believe that I had some control over this, that it would be over when I wanted it to be over. I told myself it would pass in the spring. Spring, a time for renewal, a time for hope.

I learned that anxiety could be controlled through breathing and medications like Valium. I could talk myself down from it and it would eventually pass. I learned that avoiding one's feelings can result in anxiety, that episodes like these carry a lesson.

Wow, it had been stuffing my feelings of abandonment the day of the dinner party. It was repressing my feelings in general and being in denial of just about everything that brought this on. Feelings unexpressed: that I could relate to. It had all been too much for me, and I'd broken into *a million pieces.*

I had survived my flipping-out episode—but there was more to it. . . .

Yes, I *was* alive, but the jury was still out on whether or not I'd done something permanently to damage my mind or if I was crazy or not. And since I wouldn't go to a professional; I *alone* had become the physician, therapist *and* juror, I *alone* would figure this thing out. But what did I learn?

Stay away from pot. After my episode, you couldn't have forced me to smoke or do anything remotely hallucinogenic.

Still I chastised myself thinking, '*I must be some kind of sensitive, weak-minded person. Why me?*'

Why did I flip out, while the others continued to party on? Everyone around me handled drugs. Why couldn't I?

Eventually, I began to see that my drug consumption standards were based what *other* people did, the *capacity* of others and what other people expected of me.

Maybe it was time to check my standards?

I would have to respect my own limits. After all how important was keeping up with the heavy hitters, any way.

Lessons learned: I learned to look for the lesson in everything.

Feelings, depression and anxiety are great teachers. I learned to speak up. I learned how *terribly* unsafe it was for me to keep my feelings suppressed and how important it was to *express* myself. I began to take a bit of a moral stand, about the drugs at least. Maybe I wasn't quite as much fun and a bit more serious but I began to have a greater sense of what was good for me and what wasn't and a greater awareness of what was going on around me. I had a new sense of impending danger and became more careful, about drugs, about risky situations, about everything.

Most of my anxiety had abated but fear always lurked in the back of my mind. Could this happen again—maybe there was something inherently wrong with me, maybe I was prone to this kind of thing. I began to carry Valium around in a sterling, capsule-shaped holder in the tiny waistband pocket of my jeans, but I rarely put them to use. Just knowing they were there gave me some security. When anxiety started creeping in, I'd use the calming methods I'd acquired during the breakdown, breathing in and out, concentrating on my breath only and not my thoughts, praying, using affirmations, and promising myself this would eventually be over.

Much later, Jim would say, "If someone in our crowd had wanted to jump off a bridge, Jane would have been the one there to stop them, saying, '"No, No." Safety became a big concern for me. I never wanted to be that frightened again. I became the *guardian* of not only myself but others.

Something about my role as guardian of other people and situations felt very familiar, even as ignoring my own needs felt—hmmm, very familiar. Again, vaguely, I began to see I was often in the *savior* role.

Adhering to more conventional accepted standards of conduct started to look good to me, and I wanted those around me to do the same. The hard-won lessons I gained from these events were mine alone, however, and no one else's. So there was no real saving anyone, no controlling anyone else's craziness; not Jim's or anyone else's, savior or not, but I sure gave it a good try.

The insanity continued. To say that I had Post Traumatic Stress Disorder would have been an understatement. My childhood, the addictions of others, along with the emotional stress and abandonment issues that continued in my marriage, had all pretty much done me in.

These months changed me. No longer meek, I began

to speak up every chance I got. It was awkward at first and I'm sure it came off that way. No longer a pushover, I began to be viewed as "not as compliant." Maybe so, but I wasn't chancing another breakdown. It wasn't long before I started to feel normal again. Not much changed with my relationship with Jim. But this long, self searching episode increased *my* self-awareness.

Some time later that spring, I got a call from a friend. "Meet me at the Logan Inn at five for a drink. I have a friend from Chicago I think you should meet."

Susan had recently moved to the area with a degree in Horticultural Science and the intention of starting a land-scape design firm at her beautiful farm outside of New Hope.

She, Jim, and I took to each other immediately. We went out to the bars together and hosted lots of dinner parties at the farm. Susan also had boyfriends and she liked the girls. We adored her.

Early on Susan confided in us her interest in women and her struggle to find acceptance. We all had secrets and denial. I was no longer in denial, but I was still not discussing anything that was happening with anyone but Jim and Susan. I felt pressure to come to some resolution regarding my own sexuality; after all, gay people in New Hope had certainly accepted their identity, why couldn't I?

Susan's past was very similar to my own and like almost everyone I knew at the time, she had a rough time coming to terms with her sexuality. Yet, she was able to move on and claim her stake on what she later described to me as "the Kinsey Report continuum".

What was I exactly?

By now I was honest enough with myself to admit I had feelings for women and they were *not* going away. While I was attracted, I wasn't ready to throw it all in. I began to understand that I could be attracted to both men and women. It was possible for that to be okay.

In my relationship with Jim, even with everything that was going on with him, I remained loyal. I could never see myself cheating and still remain in the marriage. Our relationship was tenuous at best. To say I was confused would have been true.

It was going to be a wild night, starting with drinks at our place, dinner at Odette's, and then off to whatever might present itself. Odette was in rare form. She always dined at a table near the entrance and the piano bar, with her two gorgeous standard, black, French Poodles and a gay boyfriend or two. When going to Odette's you didn't just walk in the door, you made an *entrance*.

"Hello darlings. Bon jour, Bon jour," she would say with

a flourish. That's *if* she liked you and lucky for us she did. She adored us. She often said to me, "Darling, you are the only one in New Hope who could run Odette's or have a restaurant like this." I didn't understand what it was about me or why she would say this, nor did I see it as prophetic, but I knew she saw something in me that she liked.

Odette was a tough as she was elegant and she didn't like everyone. She'd been known to call the customers she didn't like, "Bores, fucking idiots," in her grand French accent. Her accent somehow softened the blow.

After Odette's we continued on to the Prelude, a local gay bar with a jukebox and hysterical drag shows.

Now it was the next afternoon. It was a hangover kind of day where only *crashing* would do. We'd carried on, had lots of drinks and been crazy—our group. We thought we owned the night life in New Hope. We were at the top. . . a bunch of great friends who did everything together.

So, it was our group: Jeremy, a great friend and killer good- looking young Renaissance man and playboy of sorts, (Susan's boyfriend,) a couple of her New York, gay-model girl friends, and Jim and I who had gone to Odette's the evening before.

The next afternoon, I stopped in at the farm to check on what had happened and what we'd gotten away with. How much had we drunk and what about the drugs? But my reason for stopping wasn't just about our evening. I needed to talk to someone. I needed help.

Hanging out in her bedroom, Susan lounged on a fox throw, while I sat on Pratesi sheets at the foot of the bed.

We were great friends, not lovers, although I loved her. No, actually I was insane for her. She was so special I couldn't imagine myself with her and I knew I wasn't on her radar. She liked them "butch," and I wasn't. At this point she had not only come out, she'd become a true sexual pioneer. She did whatever her fantasy dictated, and it appeared her fantasies were many and varied.

"I saw you talking with Christine last night," she said. "Didn't I see you two leave for a bit?"

"We went out to smoke a cigarette," I shrugged.

"Nothing happened. I'm not sure how I am with all of that. I don't want to mess things up any more than they are already." I couldn't help but reminisce about my times with Suzi.

"What do you think, Susan?" I asked." I have the feelings, the desires, so does that make me gay? What about my feelings for men? You like men and women. How do you manage? I like both, but it bothers me that one side of me has been mostly unexpressed."

"It's on a continuum, I think," she replied, lounging back on pillows.

"Sounds odd maybe, but some are more gay than others. Some can have both men and women. Some have no choice. My advice is if you can avoid it, do. I've had a rough time accepting all of this, myself."

I knew she had. It wasn't easy to accept this thing, much less come out. Yet at this point in her life she was the most *out* person I knew. She'd had lots of women lovers, experimented, loved the men and they loved her. At this time I'd have to say she was finally free. Maybe the coke helped.

I've thought of her advice often and followed it for years, justifying my avoidance of further acting on my desires. I liked the broadness of her answer, not absolute, totally forgiving. I got that as a person my way will be determined by my needs, not by definitions. There was freedom in her answer, this thinking. I realized I am an evolving person and what was true for me on that day might not be true in a month or a year.

I would stay the course; although I would remain teetering somewhere on the continuum.

Things were getting crazier and crazier as time went on. Bad things were happening to our friends.

Just outside of our group, friends were flipping out,

sometimes there was violence when jealousy took over, there were bar fights and tragic drunk-driving incidents. The police drug-searched the house at Susan's farm after huge party. It was early morning when the police arrived and lucky for us, Susan had hidden the pot in her robe. Close one.

At a foundational level, we were no longer the kids we used to be. Our gang somehow had the savvy to know just when to leave a scene before any big trouble started up.

The truth was, for all my willingness to try new things, I was actually *a lightweight*. That's party talk for someone who can't handle their liquor or drugs the way their wilder friends can and that was *me*. After all, I'd had an emotional break-down which made me fragile. I no longer had the stamina I'd once possessed. The problem was, I kept trying.

I knew better.

Alcoholism ran deep in my family and I was wary from the beginning. Every time I let go and did too much, there was a *huge* price to pay. I was the child of an alcoholic and I had become a sharp detective. I could smell booze on someone's breath a mile away and could detect personality changes in a second. I was now beginning to detect them in myself. Now that scared me.

Meanwhile, big changes were happening with Jim. The volumes of amphetamines were taking over, big time. He was getting higher all the time. When high he could really let go and not in a calm way. Revved up, he was cruising right past me at top speed. Feeling completely alone, I was no longer in denial.

One afternoon, I sat on the back step of our first little house in New Hope, talking to our friend Bill. The party and Jim were inside.

I confided in Bill that for my whole life I'd been looking for family. I told him a little about my childhood struggles, how alone I felt and how I never wanted that again.

"Bill, I'm so afraid. Jim and I aren't getting along. He's mad at me all the time, so angry. When he parties, he changes and it frightens me. Why is he like this? What can I do. I really don't even *like* him when he's high."

He listened as I told him I had hoped Jim and I would be a family that stuck together through thick and thin. Jim was changing. He had been *my* big, loveable teddy bear. Now, he was no longer the guy that I married and I was pretty sure he was no longer mine. He was possessed by something else. This guy took drugs indiscriminately. Whatever was offered, he took. This was some *other* guy, a guy who had lost control of himself. My teddy bear was full of rage. My teddy bear was gone.

Bill surprised me. I had sought understanding and

compassion from him that day. But what I got was something else.

"That's just Jimmy. He's fine."

Now I could see I wasn't getting understanding or support from *him* anymore. He, too, had changed.

Now I it became abundantly clear that I was more alone in this thing than I had thought.

Alcohol had its way with my father, changing him from fun loving into a scary, mean and raging man from whom I was desperate to escape.

This scenario was repeating itself. I had come to know intrinsically when a level of intolerability had been reached. There was no turning back.

Like my mother I saw marriage as a commitment. As a child I would beg my mother to leave my father. She just couldn't do it. Leaving someone you love isn't easy. My father's addictions and wild side, my mother's denial, fear, illusions and loyalty—both of those habit patterns were at *my own* core. Horrified, I realized their behaviors were becoming my own. And I was trapped. I hoped I'd have the strength to somehow scratch my way out.

That day, talking with Bill, I felt like I really had nowhere to go, even though it looked to some like I was on top of the heap, there was no denying it, I was *totally* lost. The bottom was falling out. The safety of the relationship was proving to be gravely false. In many ways I'd known what I was getting myself into, I'd had no idea how deep this would go. Now, suddenly, it was entirely too much for me.

Shame encompassed me. I'd been so clueless and so amazingly out of touch. Fear and shame ruled me then and following my mother's lead, I worried what people would think. Not just about Jim, but about me, too. I was trained by the best. I'd grown up to worry about everything, including "what the neighbors would think."

We'd married so young. So much was unexpressed. I was naive and so thoroughly embarrassed that my husband was deciding to leave me for the drugs and to be free. Our vision of our life together was seriously not the same. He wanted to something else. I was losing my best friend, my lover and my partner and he was all I had. I felt like a fool, an extremely embarrassed fool.

Later, I would see this very differently. Then I was devastated and ashamed. I cried for weeks. Now, if my husband left me under the same circumstances, I'd realize it wasn't about me and understand that there are other forces at work. I wasn't a fool and Jim wasn't a bad person but it sure seemed that way at the time. Really we were the same, two sides of the same coin.

I was playing my part, doing my best, doing what I could, doing what I knew with what little information I had acquired at the time.

Something had to give.

Chapter 9

JIM AND I had a painful break-up at least it was for me. He wanted to leave, but I still believed it would be possible for him to change and somehow we could work it out. He didn't see it that way nor did he want to try. With all the things that had happened to me, this by far was the most devastating.

Abandoned.

I had been abandoned and I had no inner resources with which to cope.

We sold the contents of the store and the house and moved, at least for the summer, to East Hampton to live with Susan. What? I know. Crazy—right?

As bizarre as that seemed, all of us under the same roof, it was the just the buffer zone I needed. That little bit of time in transition helped me cope with eventuality of completely breaking off with Jim. I could feel the day approaching. My gut turned every time I thought about it. I felt unsteady and at a complete loss. I'd come to the Hampton's to be with my friends, but still I was all alone. We all seemed to go our own way out there. I once again, had been reaching out for closeness, togetherness and family and I wasn't getting it I was *gasping* for air.

I was the sinking ship this time. I'd have to let go of the things I thought would save me. There was *no* life preserver. I wouldn't be going gently into my future, cushioned by the stability of my friends. I would have to do this thing alone.

It wasn't till after the summer when they went back to the farm or the city that I began to build a new life on my own and look elsewhere for friends and support. Jim was gone, they all were.

All summer I'd worked at a jewelry store in East Hampton making absolutely *no* money. Now I had to find a place to live and a *real* job to pay for it. I needed *at least* enough money to keep myself afloat.

When Susan left after the summer season, along with her friends, the truth was I had no connections in that world until the next season. I would have to make new friends and work a winter job with the locals. The *locals*. . . I had no clue who *they* were, what they were like or how to meet them. I was left to fend for myself, both economically and more terrifying than that, worse than that, socially. They were gone. *Gone*.

How was I going to make it now? Who *was* I on my own, not defined or propped up by the presence of other people? This was *it* and come hell or high water. Was I going to make it? I would have to find out. What is it like to all of a sudden feel like to be a 'nobody.' I can tell you for sure, not good at all.

East Hampton was and still is beautiful. It is chic, artsy, rich and smart. The Hamptons were all about accomplishment, money and good looking people. I might have been some of those things, some of the time, at least outwardly back in Bucks County. But who was I here and on the inside?

My first restaurant job was at a place called Shazam in East Hampton. I lied to the owners, David and Steven, embellishing the work experience I'd gotten at the Ranch. I'd had waitressing experience, worked in the kitchen, oh and I could *bartend*, too. I got the job.

Allie, the Queen of Shazam, and the E.H. funky crowd, was my work savior. Allie taught me how to serve. I knew she *suspected* that I had *very little* experience but went along with my little charade. Trailing behind her for a few nights, watching her take orders, recommend and serve wines gave me the start I needed. Allie was social with some of the East Hampton summer folks and could chat it up with the best of them. She was New York savvy, so funky and so cool.

She and most of her friends worked in the city in the winter as stylists, entertainers, bartenders, designers. They hung out at the primo, funky, cool, bar in Amagansett called Stephen Talkhouse. It was at the Talkhouse where I met Shamus, the super popular, curly-haired, very smart, Donovan look alike bartender. Ten years older, Shamus had a girlfriend who was having an affair. So all things being equal, I seized the opportunity.

Shamus and I had a mostly on and sometimes off thing going for the next several years. In some ways this was crazy, and in other ways an affair with an unavailable man was exactly what I needed. Not a perfect or highly functioning relationship, but fun nevertheless. I adored him.

Shamus was a huge drinker. He told me once,

"The booze is my lover."

"Dewars rocks, Coke back please."

I followed with, "Rusty Nail," the only thing remotely like scotch that I could tolerate. I know, intense. I hated

Scotch but the added sweetness of the Drambuie softened it a bit.

Now Shamus had something I liked. He was a bright, charming, brooding Irish lad—America meets Ireland. I'd meet him at the bar toward the end of his shift at the Talkhouse, where we'd hang out, close up and head off to my house or Cavenaro's, (the hard drinking, working-class bar catering mostly to firemen at the crack of dawn and later in the day to potato farmers and Bonac* fishermen.) Cavenaro's was frequented by the likes of Jackie Kennedy Onassis, Billy Joel, Alan Alda and Jackson Pollack. I loved the characters. Shamus and I conversed with the best of them, delighting in their accents, mannerisms, and stories, all while I delighted in his. These feelings I had for Shamus were the closest thing I'd had to how I felt in the early days of my romance with Jim.

Allie was in charge at Shazam. I had really lucked out meeting her, I thought. She was super cool and had great connections and lots of friends. She was kind and generous with her friendship and her time. Allie showed me so much about the restaurant business, enough to help me fake it till I made it.

---

* **Bonac.** A very local name for the town of East Hampton taken after the Accabonac Creek that runs through the area. A Bonacker is a local inhabitant who is descended from the original settlers who arrived in the area in the early 1600's.

It was at Shazam that I learned how to work in a professional kitchen and made the decision to seriously pursue a career in the restaurant business. The French chef, Jean de Mol's, resume was impressive. Jean had worked in New York with amazing chefs like Andre Soltner of Lutece fame. He was a tough guy, French chef, who threw his weight around in the kitchen. Jean was brutal with his commies (trainees,) but not so much with me. He wasn't the most patient person, nevertheless he shared with me many techniques needed to produce classical French cuisine. I was on my way.

This was all very different. I'd been at the top or close to it back in Bucks County. I had my business, my friends, my house and my reputation, such as it was. Here I was, a nobody with a Capitol 'N', and boy did it hit me big-time. I'd have to struggle and do all this by myself. I had no relative, friend, connected person to help me or make me look good. I saw how dependent I had become on others, not only for my survival but for my identity and reputation.

Surrounding myself with successful, connected people had always worked for me. It worked until I, too, became successful and connected in Bucks County. I liked being around extraordinary people, I respected them and they made me look good. If I hung out with someone and they were attractive, smart, rich or famous, or even infamous, I thought it would reflect well on me by making me look more interesting and make me look important. Now, in the Hamptons, I could see the *shallowness* of it all. If I didn't have any depth inside of me, I'd have to use yours.

The need to live from a deeper place within myself lay just ahead.

A year after settling into the Hamptons, I began to have serious health issues. It started after a huge bout with the flu. I was having difficulty breathing, there was pain in my chest and I was exhausted. If I walked a flight of stairs, it felt like I'd hiked a mountain. The X-rays taken of my chest showed I had a mass on my left lung and now I needed a biopsy. There were two possibilities and only a biopsy would determine what was going on. It would either be Hodgkin's disease or a rare immune disorder called Sarcoidosis. The recovery rate for Hodgkin's disease was very low. I prayed for Sarcoidosis and I got my answer.

Thirty Six stitches later under my left breast, the removal of a huge lymph node, another near the collarbone and some under my arm proved it was not Hodgkin's disease. Even though Sarcoidosis wasn't a great diagnosis, I've been forever grateful.

I had been given my first gift of seeing how precious life really is. I became determined to live life to the very fullest.

The prescription for the management of Sarcoidosis is generally Prednisone, which I took for the next three years. I'd always been sensitive to hormones and steroids. I knew that from always having to take the lowest dose of birth control. But now the amount I needed was huge and there was no reducing it. Prednisone began to have it's way with me. To say I was jacked up and speed-like for those three years from the massive doses of Prednisone would in fact be *true*.

Even though I'd had my first brush with the need to go deeper, I slid back immediately into my old ways. The Prednisone was like jet fuel. It made me want more of everything: food, sex, everything. I became a promiscuous, ravenous, partying fool. Though I was still having an affair with Shamus with obviously no commitment, I was free to play around.

Shazam eventually closed after a few seasons. I got a job working at the Coach House on Montauk Highway in East Hampton with Sandy McCoy. It wasn't fancy, just a pretty good lunch and dinner house and Sandy was in charge. Now, not only did I have my friend Allie, but now I'd met another great person.

Sandy was a hard working, local girl with a great reputation in the restaurant business. Everyone said if there were ever a saint, Sandy was it. She worked hard, had two little girls to take care of and she did a good job of it. Sandy's crowd was a new bunch of hard drinking, restaurant people who in no time became my crowd as well: local, fun, crazy and wild party people.

We partied nightly after work and on the weekend. Every Monday as many as fifteen of us met for lunch and drinks at a local restaurant. We dubbed ourselves the Out to Lunch Bunch and we certainly were. The festivities began around noon and very rarely did we get home before dawn.

Like most restaurant people we worked super hard and we'd hang out for awhile at one of the bars until relaxed enough to go home. And if that zenned-out moment hadn't yet arrived, we'd just continue through the night. . . somewhere.

One of the guys in our crowd was local bartender boy, Tommy Miller. Tommy charmed the crowd with his talents for humor, sarcasm, insults and crazy antics, drinking and doing whatever it took to get crazy. He wasn't all that nice but I must say he was entertaining. Attracted to that sort of crazy, I moved into his house in town not long after meeting him. The turning point for me with Tommy was a late evening at Bobby Van's with our Out to Lunch Bunch.

Big partying right from the start, things took a distinct downturn around ten o'clock.

It seems Tommy had an issue with the bartender, culminating in accusations and threats. I was standing at the end of the bar, trying to stay out of the way when all of a sudden, in a rage, Tommy hurled a bar stool at the bartender. Missing his intended target, it crashed squarely onto the back of my head.

I didn't see it coming and when it hit, I must have passed out cold. I found myself flat on my back, lying on the bar floor. As I came to, I felt the back of my head with my hand. There was blood all over, on my head, my hand, and on the floor.

"What happened?"

They told me. I looked around. Where was Tommy? He'd fled, nowhere to be found. I was furious. He'd gotten in his car and run, the coward. The police never showed, he needn't have run. His sister took me to the emergency room for stitches.

How could this have happened? I had just been standing there. A voice in my head tried to get through; 'things have gotten very out of hand, wrong place, wrong time and obviously the wrong crowd.'

I'd found myself in another unsafe situation of my own making. The big clue once again was; 'get the hell out of here.' Tommy never apologized or mentioned what happened, and

I knew better than to let him know what a shit I thought he was, being the shit that he truly *was*.

I soon found an apartment of my own in Sag Harbor. Now I would be the only one to blame for whatever happened to me.

The summer crowd of friends returned but this season something had changed. Things were different. 'What was it?'

At first I couldn't put my finger on it. But then, one evening, while partying at a friend's summer house, I got it, I understood, I could see clearly now what was going on.

First thing, the crowd had changed. There were some new people around, not just the nice people I'd gotten to know the summer before. These were city people with big reputations. They had a sort of scary aura, a mysterious aloof quality. A couple of the Warhol Factory crowd hung in for the late night, all night parties. They were preceded by their reputations and their fame. The sweet, fancy Ivy League crowd had now been replaced with a wilder crowd and more serious devotees of blow.

Not a part of that crowd, but an occasional guest, I'd go because a few of my old summer friends were there. The favorite thing to do, besides the coke, was to expound brilliantly *ad infinitum and ad nauseum* while obsessively recording every *precious, brilliant word* for posterity. This was a Warhol thing. The conversations were convoluted, intense and I wonder if they made any sense at all when played back. It was all beyond me. I didn't know what anyone was talking about anymore and I didn't care.

Nothing made sense, not *these* people or their conversations, not the *affair* with the boyfriend, not the lovers, certainly not the Out to Lunch Bunch, Tommy or the partying *and* my health was failing.

It was all too much and it was wearing on me. I began to *hate* the life I had created.

What *was* working for me was the restaurant thing. I'd kept my eyes open, I was learning and studying every moment I worked with Chef Jean. Sandy and Allie showed me what I needed to know about the front of the house. I was yearning to take on brand new challenges of the *restaurant kind.*

I just couldn't stay in East Hampton any longer. Once again, I'd taken everything to the limit. I *can* say, I had more fun in the Hamptons than anywhere ever but enough was enough. I couldn't take it anymore.

I had no clue where I should go, but I prayed, *so* hard.

Please God, please, get me out of here . . .

Chapter 10

PRAYING TO GET OUT of the Hamptons? Indeed
I was.

Again, I'd had enough and needed an escape. At some
point it began to dawn on me that I really needed to start
looking at this pattern of mine—making poor choices,
impulsive decisions, taking everything to the limit and then
always finally desperately needing to escape. But acting on
that thought could wait. Meanwhile I would be on the move
again. Once more, I had reached my personal gamut of wan-
ton behavior. I was done. It was time to move on.

Was it the party scene that made me run? Yes and
something else. I was really hungering for a more peaceful,
familiar setting. It was time to take my culinary resume,

experience and training to the next level, but where? I'd prayed. Now I would have to wait.

One evening, my cousin John called while I was in East Hampton to tell me,

"The Ranch is in the planning stages of a new restaurant. I'll be managing the front of the house."

I jumped at the thought of the *possible outside* chance they might want me to join them.

I asked,

"Would you like me to design the menu and work on the project for the summer?"

"Yes, definitely."

'What?' Fantastic, I couldn't believe it.

Being back at the Ranch and spending time with the staff and my cousins was amazing. I don't think they realized just how important they were to me. They were my only semblance of family and I really needed them in my life. I headed up to Lake George with my dog Alice, my VW van full of my things and the funds to get me there.

The Powder Horn Room was the first restaurant John and I opened and it was to be the first 'open to the public' restaurant at the Ranch which had and still has a modified American plan dining concept for the vacationing guests. John was to be the host and I, the chef. I was so grateful that I got to express my culinary talents while creating a menu that was well received. The public came and the restaurant did pretty well that season and we had such a fun time creating and running the place.

I set up my things in the bunk house where I'd stayed some fourteen years before. The bunk house was definitely rattier but other than that not much had changed. I worked, dated a bit, went out to the bars, hung out with cousins on the lake, hit the track with them in Saratoga and felt great about every bit of it. I wasn't as grateful as I should have been but I felt as home and as loved as I ever would anywhere.

The season in Lake George only lasts so long, so, after the summer John and I headed off to the Breakers in Palm Beach where I'd often stayed with my parents, *as a guest*. It was at the Breakers where we both found jobs, he as a waiter and me as a chef. Now I would be a chef at *this* prestigious establishment.

What a change though. I was told employees had no access to the dining rooms, bars or any part of the front of the house, not even on a day off. Staff arrived and left through the back only. I was appalled.

'Didn't they know who I was? '

Still I was enormously excited. I believe I was to be the first woman chef at the Breakers. I held the incredibly *exhausting* position of Vegetable Chef on the line. I was preparing vegetable side dishes for up to twelve hundred guests nightly in season. It was hot, hot, and hot in the often one hundred twenty degree, football-field-sized kitchen. The demand for perfection was intense. I was a boiling-hot-red faced-cooking fool in this line of all-male chefs and me.

I'd been warned the highly experienced, European trained, macho chefs would most likely have an attitude with me, but not so. They were a great bunch of guys from all over the world willing to show me the ropes. The Food and Beverage Manager was another story. He was a mean and nasty, little tyrant who tortured the staff with his insults, especially the Hispanic women in the pantry. It was hard to watch him demean them, by yelling and embarrassing them in front of the rest of the staff. We stood there at our positions, waiting for our own admonitions.

I'd stand there glaring at him with a look that *screamed*, "Go ahead, try it."

The Executive Chef and I however, became great buddies. He was so impressed that I'd agreed to chef on the line, and I was so grateful he had allowed me to do it.

When I applied I'd said, "I don't want to do the traditional women's jobs, like pantry work or prep. I'd like to be on the line." Miraculously, he hired me.

When it was unbearably hot in the kitchen, when I thought I'd faint from the heat, when the pots were so heavy I'd almost collapse and when the pressure to produce very quickly, perfectly presented food would exhaust me. . . I'd sometimes wonder what I'd been thinking to want this job. But I did love it. The Chefs became my friends, even taking me to the bar in West Palm where the other Palm Beach Chefs hung out after work, late at night.

I liked the entire scene but it was pretty lonely living in West Palm Beach. I was in a good position at The Breakers. I knew how good all of this would look at my resume but as my thirtieth birthday rolled around I felt a kind of internal shame.

'Shouldn't I be more established by now? Shouldn't I be more settled?'

After all I was now a vagabond seasonal chef with no roots.

But soon the winter season would be over and I would head north to New Hope for a chef's job at resort called La Camp. . . I would be chef in my own kitchen and in New Hope where I *knew* people.

New Hope had at least twenty restaurants at the time and I thought, 'what better place?'

But it took real courage to go back there. I was so horribly embarrassed about the breakup with Jim; at this point I was certain everyone knew my story. Things that were personal were no longer secret, and of course my change in status from the pretty shopkeeper, party person who never stopped, to a hard working dedicated chef with a fairly impressive resume was a huge change. But New Hope was my home and I loved it.

La Camp had a fairly young hetero/bi party crowd that mixed well with the everyday ancient bar crowd of gay men. Even with this younger crowd, the scene soon became tiresome to me with the *same* people on the *same* bar stools every night.

My friend Mary Kay called the place *'sheets.'* She joked that at night when they closed, they would just cover up the patrons sitting on their stools with *sheets*. In the morning they'd be uncovered and ready for a new day.

There is a time for everything and this time in my life was going to be about getting it together in more ways than one.

There was a reason I'd been praying all the time. I could see I was going nowhere fast the way I had been carrying on in the Hamptons and I didn't want to continue with that in New Hope. I became almost hermit like and *completely* career focused. I read everything I could about Culinary History and Foreign Cuisines and Julia Child.

Julia taught America the joys of French Cuisine while breaking down the complexities. After Julia came had the more modern but not necessarily better Cuisine Minceur, California Cuisine and New American followed by World Cuisine. I studied them all, meeting the Chefs in New York, California and the Key's, traveling to their restaurants, copying their techniques until I developed my own.

All the while I was still scoping out the restaurant scene in New Hope. Mother's was *the* most popular restaurant where my new friend Marco Coelho worked. Marco was from a Portuguese New Bedford, Massachusetts clan who owned fishing boats. He was an amazing friend. He and I spent a great deal of time together in P-Town having fun with his friends and going to the beach and bars.

It was Marco who suggested to the owners of Mothers in New Hope; Stephanie and Joe, that I join their team in the kitchen. It wasn't long before I was working with Joe as Mother's Chef. Meanwhile, the restaurant was doing outrageously well.

Mother's was *famous* and the *hottest* place going. Crowds waited for over an hour to get in on the weekends. Stephanie and her morning staff put out gorgeous breakfasts while Joey and his gang rocked it at dinner, while my crew and I prepped our asses off supplying them with the necessary sauces, meats, veggies they needed. Creating Mothers very unique menu was our job and we loved doing it. Known for being a fun place with *attitude*; the gay waiters and gorgeous waitresses doled it out with great humor.

Our dress code was 'Bathing Suits to Ball Gowns.' And yes, the food was amazing. So amazing that chefs from all over made Mother's a must do stop.

One day, much to my delight, Julia Child and her husband Paul stopped in for lunch. They were visiting Paul's brother Charles who lived up the road. We were *over the top* thrilled. Julia was lovely and appreciated the attention and the specially prepared lunch we served them which included my Curry Burger with Apple and Pear Chutney. Julia and I chatted for a bit.

I asked her about her first cookbook, *Mastering the Art of French Cooking.*

"When you wrote, *Mastering the Art of French Cooking* and how did you find a publisher?" I needed to know because I had a cookbook on the back burner.

I told her that my book was about Duck, incorporating a unique way of preparing it—oven braising while keeping the skin crispy at the same time. Julia listened, seemed interested and said we could talk; she would like to take a look at it when I was finished.

I said "Thank you, thank you."

After sending off several chapters and finding there was no interest in a book featuring such a laborious and messy item such as duck, I chose to discontinue writing the book.

It was around this time that I visited my parents in Saint Petersburg, Florida. Much to my surprise, Daddy was sober and had been for awhile. He was having health issues and was scheduled for two operations to be performed at the same time; hiatal hernia and gallbladder. He was afraid and had begun a big weight loss regime along with not drinking, hoping to be thinner and healthier for the surgeries.

We had a pretty good visit. I left and didn't think about his operation for awhile until I got a call from my mother late one afternoon.

"Souvey, Daddy has had his operations and he's not doing well. It's been too much for his heart and he is struggling. You better call him."

As she told me, I thought.

'I've completely forgotten about the surgeries. Why? I should have remembered. I should have called. I've been so involved with my own crazy life...'

"Hello. Daddy, is that you? Are you all right?" His voice was stressed.

"Honey, I can't talk with you now. They are giving me an enima."

And strangely, those were his last words to me... Losing my father like that, so suddenly, and without having been there for him when he might have needed me, felt awful. But after the shame, another overwhelming feeling surfaced immediately, *relief.*

I knew admitting these feelings of relief would make me appear callous, had I shared them with anyone. Of course I felt bad for him and his struggle at the end, but there was more.

I thought, 'Well, *that's* finally over.'

There would be, *for sure*, no more tortuous episodes. My mother would be free and on many levels, so would I. Mother and I talked about our feelings, how we honestly felt about his passing. Not surprisingly, she also was relieved. We worked together on creating a lovely memorial service and brunch for family and friends at the condo in Florida.

✳ ✳ ✳

Daddy,

I was so angry with you when Mother called me from Florida one weekend while I was at boarding school.

Mother and I would chat every few weeks.

I'd always ask, "How are you doing? What's going on with Daddy?"

This time she was crying.

"He's been drinking all the time. He's so angry. . . I don't know what to do. I was relaxing on our terrace with a book, trying to get away from him, while he was in a drunken rage in the living room. Screaming and so drunk, he started throwing his shoes at the sliding glass doors between us to get my attention."

As she told me, I felt powerless in my inability to help her and so angry with you.

I thought, 'So many years of this. . . she was just trying to have a little peace away from you. You had to break through the silence she craved and deserved, that anyone deserves.' My heart sank that day and it stayed sunk until the day you died.

She was just wanted some peace and you would never let her have it.

What was it? I know you were an alcoholic. You ruined our lives and *never* acknowledged it. Not once. Not even once.

For many years I thought that if you loved me you would stop drinking but you didn't and that was a rotten feeling. Maybe you were having blackouts. I didn't know. Of course I didn't know. I didn't know anything about alcoholism. All I knew was that you were one and I hated *it*. But I did love *you*.

You know I never wanted to be like Mother, so vulnerable and weak. There were many things I loved about you. One was your wry sense of humor. You knew the angles, had just the right quip. You were brilliant with your words, succinctly letting people know in just a few words what the deal was. I adored that invulnerability.

It turned out, I was the lucky one. Much luckier than Mother; I got to leave. Boarding school was my salvation. As grateful as I was to get out of there I did feel bad for Mother, who remained. So I had mixed feelings about leaving for boarding school. I knew it was the best thing that could ever happen for me but knowing that she was left to fend for herself and deal with your drinking made me sad.

So, I'm sorry Daddy I wasn't there for you after your operation but it is perfectly understandable. . . You had not been in my consciousness for years. . .

* * *

Meanwhile, back in New Hope at Mother's, my career was headed in a very positive direction but there still were challenges. Old habits die hard. It was the height of the cocaine era everywhere and *big time* in New Hope. The party scene was hot but I'd had more than enough already. I was a little older than the party crowd at this point, thirty one, and I had moved on for the most part. Cocaine dominated and the users seemed to be getting thinner and thinner not to mention crazier and crazier. Meanwhile one of my other addictions took on a life of its own.

My old food addiction began to accelerate beyond anything I'd experienced before. I wasn't doing drugs and my sex life was stagnant so my fallback was food. I'd been given the reins at Mothers and I ran with it. It was all about food; reading and testing recipes, studying cuisine trends, menu planning, menu writing, instructing the cooks how to prep and execute the menu and of course *my* down fall, overeating.

I was getting bigger and bigger and the worst part was I didn't give a damn, another addiction I couldn't stop and it frightened me. I was embarrassed by my size. I'd gained 60 pounds. My eating was completely out of control and I looked it. I'd never been this big before. I remember looking down at my thighs while in bed one evening and I couldn't believe how enormous they were. How had I allowed this to happen?

Once I'd finally emerged from the River of Denial. My weight issue really needed to be addressed. I put myself on what I called *My Spa Program* of exercise, healthy fruits and vegetables, protein, smoothies, massages, facials, chiropractors and even a therapist. I was willing to do almost anything to improve myself. I let my hair grow and got a great cut. It was sex that had brought me back from the seemingly unstoppable eating frenzy and the nagging realization that there was more, more to life than just food and a career.

No way was I going out with the intention of meeting someone looking the way I had. After a few months of this Spa regime I'd definitely achieved a well needed transformation. I was ready to have some fun before my *ebb had completely ebbed*.

I wanted it to be *flow time* once again, back to more *action* and more *life* in my life. Jim and I were still separated and I wanted to play around. I wasn't waiting for my hotshot friends to return, although I loved it when they did. Physically I was ready to move on but some things were still unresolved, strangely I found it almost impossible to move forward.

I was driven by a feeling of responsibility to my better self and an attraction to women, yet I was completely paralyzed—as attracted as I was, I realized I was afraid of women. I'd hadn't had any idea just how afraid I was. I felt just couldn't trust them. I knew these feelings came from the neglect and mistrust of my mother. At a horrible, frustrating crossroad, I wanted to have a relationship with a woman or at least date, but I couldn't move forward. I felt like something was really wrong with me, and there was. I had read about problems like this. People who had these issues are labeled sexually dysfunctional. Dysfunctional? The word literally screamed out to me from the page. What the hell? I felt like a freak. . .

I thought, 'What kind of person is dysfunctional?' Not functioning like the rest of humanity managed to do with such a natural, basic instinct as sex?. Now I knew the reason for my overeating, I had taken this on and I had eaten over it.

Working through this in therapy, I got to see that I needed to face my truth and my truth was, I was attracted to women. I was a woman who had loved men. I was me in all of my complexities and I could, with help, work through my fears.

First thing; I needed to start dating, not just affairs. Second; I needed to find out if the lifestyle was for me. I had my doubts. Third; I needed to decide, or did I?

I felt I *could* make a choice and still not have it be a cop out. The continuum theory said I could be *anywhere* on it, didn't it? This wasn't going to be instantaneous. It would be a *process*.

It might have looked like I was deciding to be *gay* one day and *straight* another but that's *not* the story. The story is that I was just working it through and I had to come to some resolve about it.

There was pressure; pressure from some of my gay friends to basically, 'admit it, you are gay and from straight people, 'you're not gay. We can't see you as gay.'

And the truth is, I didn't know. I knew I had to find out. I seemed to be both, and at the time that wasn't a very widely accepted concept in the Gay community, or any community, really. But who was I trying to please?

The idea that a person can all of a sudden decides to have gay or perhaps bi-sexual feelings floors me. Does anyone just *decide* to have sexual feelings of any kind? Straight people don't all of a sudden *decide* to feel turned on by the opposite sex.

News flash, Those of us who are attracted to *whomever*, didn't just choose it. It just friggin' started up, like from nowhere. Gay people cannot change their sexual orientation just because someone or some section of society thinks their mere existence is an annoyance or even a sin.

I had worked through all of it in my mind. I would be open to possibilities and those possibilities would be based on what was right for me and for *no one else*. And that is exactly when I had what I consider to be a Spiritual Awakening.

At that very moment, the most amazing, incredible, *miraculous* thing happened. I was surrounded by what felt like the *warmest cushion* of air. I actually could physically *feel* this, this cushion of beautiful, soft, tender warmth around me. For the first time in my life, *I felt loved.* What was it? It certainly wasn't coming from me. I didn't have the power to create such a thing. . .

The feeling lasted for weeks. I knew I was being guided, and in the right direction. I knew it was now *spiritually right* to accept this and all parts of the complexity that is me.

Where would I take this new loving acceptance? I could now move forward with a feeling of freedom and validation.

Free to be me.

Chapter II

I HAD JUST STARTED moving on with the dating scene when something temporarily brought everything to a standstill. I got a call from my mother,

"Souvey, I have breast cancer. I've decided to have chemo and a double mastectomy."

We talked. . .

I think I'll be okay after the operation and the chemo. Can you stay with me for a little while?"

I found myself saying,

"Of course, I will."

And I did, for almost two months. Why? Why would I do such a thing after all that had happened? Immediately I saw this as an enormous opportunity to make things good and right. Knowing this was the right thing to do, I *had* to go.

It was odd without my father there. This was a chance to make something new for ourselves, a time to get to know each other without the drama and the worrying. So, although a sad time, it was peaceful as well.

One remarkable thing about my mother was that she never complained. She just went along with everything - the illness, the tests, the seemingly unending chemo, and the nauseating side-effects.

About six months after returning to Bucks County, Mother invited me to join her on a trip to Spain, Portugal and Morocco. I think she suspected the cancer might return. This time *she* wanted to heal *us*.

Of course I looked forward to the trip. I hadn't been to any of these places and I knew the trip was just what we needed, so many questions to ask, so much to learn, so much to heal.

We met at JFK in time to catch our flight to Spain and I wasn't in the best shape.

Several nights before leaving on our trip, a group of us including the New York crowd, Marco, Jim, and I arrived at HAVANA at closing time after going to the bars. I hadn't hadn't been a big coke user but I made up for it that night.

I did my share, maybe more, apparently too much, a few lines and then more and more again.

It was then I got it.That evening I'd done enough to understand the transforming feeling of going from my usual neurotic, insecure self to instantly feeling taller, sexier and more beautiful. I felt like a million bucks and then nada, nothing. I was left with nothing but a nasty sinus infection, headache and a massive, waterfall nose for the rest of the three week trip.

We did have a wonderful trip visiting all the sites, enjoying the tours, the food and the best of all for me, Morocco. We adored the exotic, forbidden nature and the maze of alleys of the old historic medina in Marrakech, with the dress, the look and smells mired in ancient times.

Mother did seem even thinner than when I'd seen her a year ago. I wondered if she had a new diagnosis. She was quiet for much of the trip, we both were.

Mother and I healed as much as two people like us could, two people who together had been through so much, two people who didn't really know one another. I never had the courage to share with her who I really was and what I had been through. We would never be close but we had a history, love and the best intentions.

Just a few months after our return Mother called again.

The cancer had reappeared. This time in her lungs and she was scared. The prognosis wasn't good and she decided this time, "no chemo".

We needed to make plans. She offered to go to a nursing home in Florida to wait it out, but I couldn't let her do that. I asked her come live with me in Bucks County after we settled her things in Florida.

Incredibly, *at the very same time,* Jim's mom was also diagnosed with advanced stage lung cancer and was also given six to nine months. They had the same prognosis, six months to live, with or without chemo. His mom chose chemo. My mother, who realized the very low, (5%), recovery rate and the really unpleasant complications of chemo, declined.

Jim and I had been spending time together and gotten close, again. We were stunned by the news of the double diagnosis and decided to pool our efforts to help our moms while living at my house for awhile. So when my mother and I returned home from Florida, Jim moved back in with me helping me take care of my mom while running down to his mom's house to be with her. I don't know how he managed it all while still working.

As for me, it was one thing to help Mother deal with the chemo and the double mastectomy in Florida and help her move. It was an *entirely* another matter to have her in my home and watch her die. The memories of my childhood over-shadowed *everything* and I was *drowning* in a little child's feelings.. I kept thinking: 'How can I nurture someone who didn't nurture me as a child? How can I save someone who didn't save me?' It wasn't anger; it was a certain deep rooted helplessness that I was experiencing. Yet I did everything I could to make her comfortable but the way I *felt*. . . I had an overwhelming desire to run and run and never stop running. All the while, never letting her know how uncomfortable I felt.

Yet I did it. And Jim did it when I just couldn't. He was *amazingly* kind to her.

Wonderful home health aides from the church came a few times a week. This couldn't have been done without them and Jim by my side.

The saddest day for me was one, about two weeks before my mother died. She said she was in a lot of pain and the morphine wasn't helping. Mother reached for my hand. "I need to sit up but I can't do it by myself. Would you fix the pillows and help me, please."

When I gently placed my hand on the middle of her back to release the pillows, I realized she couldn't place her-self back onto the pillows by herself. Having no control, she helplessly fell back in between pillows and the bars on the hospital bed and couldn't lift herself up. I gasped in disbelief. I couldn't believe what had just happened. At that moment she had lost every ounce of strength. It was like something had just taken an enormous chunk of life force out of her. I could see the fear in her eyes. It was clear to both of us that her time was coming soon.

Watching life leave my mother was agonizing. Mother passed away in her sleep after a peaceful six month decline.

Jim's mother died two weeks later. Our mom's paths were very different. Mother had a peaceful time of it while Jim's mom suffered with a heart attack and stroke from the chemo.

Things weren't the same for us after our mothers died. We had done our best to make our mothers comfortable but after our mission had been accomplished, Jim moved out. We had held it together in a crisis but we drifted once again, back to our previous paths.

It wasn't until both of my parents passed on that I was able to really open up. Something parental had such an extremely powerful grip on me. Allow me to explore this again, this time either a bit more awareness.

What happens to a child, when they are inadvertently not parented, not nurtured, and unable to bring friends home? What happens to a child when they are treated like a burden, an embarrassment and emotionally abused?

This is what happened to me. I didn't feel wanted. I was never secure. I didn't know how to live or to *be*, meaning. I had no role models, no siblings to bounce this stuff off of. I had no clue how to react to this life of mine. I had so much wanted a brother or sister but if I'd had one I would have felt sorry for them; very telling. I'd been so unhappy. I honestly feel I've already lived my hell. It's like if I ever do another bad thing it would be alright because the penance has been paid. Yet today, I have a sense of forgiveness about everything. I know none of the things my parents did were intentionally meant to hurt me. Their parenting was simply a by-product of their own issues and I am very certain they had no idea the impact their behavior would have on me.

Always looking for channels of escape, I learned rather early that my survival depended upon *getting the hell out of there*. Being sent away to boarding school proved to be the key to my survival. I hate to imagine what might have happened had I stayed.

Some of the prejudices of my family and the Church had begun to take hold. The nuns told us it was wrong for a man to be with a man or a woman to be with a woman, even though at the time I had no idea what they were talking about.

I believed whatever they told us, except of course when they expounded innumerable times that kissing a boy was a mortal sin. Even then I saw that as *complete manipulation* on their part. So, on a child's level I thought if the Church thinks kissing a boy is a sin then what other things are they telling us that may not be true? I had to reevaluate. So many things they said seemed absurd.

It was time to find out on my own just what *I* believe I *am* a 'make the most out of a bad situation' kind of girl who wound up being a pretty good survivor. Not having been nurtured nor given tools for life, *lost*, I searched and searched, trying to find my way and not always in the best places.

Alcoholism was rampant in my family, as well as homophobia. My father's Irish side called them, "fairies or "queers"; my mother called them "fruits." I needed to find out what was true for me and what my values were. More and more, I came to see that the Church's and my parents' values were not my own. I still loved the Church, the beauty of it, the hymns, Benediction, the incense and the feelings of fervor that overwhelmed me, but these seemingly preposterous ideas were getting to me.

As I began to revise my own slate of beliefs I found myself going back to where they first took shape... Grammar school.

"You are so *queer*. That is so *queer*."

Queer was the major and highly overused word by the students of St Mark's parochial school in Peoria while I was attending.

Queer.

We had no idea. To us it meant the *other* meaning, odd, weird. To my parents, my use of the word sent up red flags.

"Do you know what that word means?"

"What word?" I was using it so often; I didn't even hear myself saying it.

"*Queer*, it means when a man loves another man."

"What?" I couldn't believe she thought I meant such a thing when *I* said it.

There was no convincing her, but I did use it a whole lot less after that. In retrospect, this taught me something about her. There was an unexpected kindness and tolerance in her explanation that still surprises me. After all she could have said many worse things, but she didn't. Mother always thought of herself as broadminded, perhaps more in theory than in reality, perhaps more in areas of race and women's equality than sexuality.

Broadminded or not, it was difficult then, as it is now, for many parents and families of those who fall outside the so-called "norm" on the continuum of sexuality to accept their children. God, in my opinion, it's hard enough for LGBTQ people to accept themselves and yet many expect those they 'come out' to, to readily accept their sexuality pretty soon after being told. Everyone wants to be accepted *as they are* in their families. Really, when you think about it, if it's a *process* for us to accept ourselves, it is also a *process* for those we love. Time takes time.

The struggle gay people were experiencing all around me was *tremendous*. The hurt and the stress *are* toxic. The suicide rate among gay men and women is shockingly large.

I wondered: 'What if I'd been able to deal with these issues much earlier?'

The fact was, struggles of any kind were un-shareable with my parents. I never felt I could tell them *anything* about who I was. Their opinions and judgments hovered over me like a dense, formidable cloud from which I was unable to escape, at least while they were alive. Even as an adult I remained stuck.

That is the *long and short of it* and may explain why I had such an enormously difficult time accepting myself and moving beyond such tremendous pressure to conform.

Much of this I came to understand through therapy and a group for children of alcoholics. Marco introduced me to his therapists in Hopewell, New Jersey who ran support groups for adult children of alcoholics. The first time I walked into a room full of other adults who had parents who were alcoholics I felt like I was home. My feelings of loneliness and depression gave way to a new sense of hope and family. In so many ways the people in these rooms seemed like the brothers and sisters I'd always wanted. Having a support group of people with the same issues open up a whole new world for me.

Here was the biggest thing: *I no longer felt alone.* This was the start I needed in my search for wholeness.

But with baby steps and a little bit of sobriety, a new awareness was creeping in. At group, they continually talked about gratitude—developing *'an attitude of gratitude.'* I couldn't understand what gratitude had to do with being a child of an alcoholic or alcoholism.

I knew I didn't have gratitude. I thought, 'There has to be something wrong with a person who has no gratitude.'

I needed to find out more and I had to admit I couldn't handle staying sober all by myself. *'Damn, I need support,'* just like I did as a child when I wanted to go to Alateen and my mother wouldn't let me to go out of fear and shame. But

I was a big girl now and she was *dead* and this time *I* needed to get *this* child inside of me some *help*.

The adult-child support group had *rules* and one of them was, *"No drinking for six weeks* while the group is in session."

They wanted us to be present in every way for the sessions, to be fully conscious and open to growth. We all agreed, and I was more than willing. I seriously wanted change. I'd been in survival mode for so long. Loneliness and depression had taken over. I really needed this group and the therapy sessions with super therapist Betty Anderson in Hopewell.

Betty was great; she had worked with people like me for years. It was like she *knew* me. I liked the attention and on some level I knew what I needed was nurturing and I got it. I was more than willing to not drink and the trade-off was well worth it.

Sometime before I began going to my new group, Marco had started sampling what AA had to offer on an occasional basis.

Marco *loved* cocaine. The coke made long hours of *extended* drinking possible.

At the time Marco was a partner at HAVANA in New Hope. The restaurants in New Hope had been up to this point all on the *quaint* side. HAVANA was far from quaint. Designed to attract a party crowd, HAVANA was at the time, more bar-nightclub than restaurant, a party place complete with bands and late hours. At the time, I was the chef at HAVANA as well as at Mother's.

Marco wasn't happy with some things that were going on at the restaurant and did he drink and drug over it? Yes, and so did we all but for different reasons. The place got crazy pretty fast with everyone carrying on, blow being sold by the regulars and an unstated free drinks for drugs exchange policy some of the bartenders had,

'I give you 3 drinks, you tip me $10 and sometimes a toot and we're even,' with nothing going in the till.

Late in the evenings or anytime no one was looking, lines were sucked up *right off the bar* and the queue for the bathrooms was out the door.Not surprisingly, sales dropped to staggering low figures. The place became horribly in debt to the government and something had to be done to save the place. Marco was in a panic and things got worse, not better.

Marco was a mess but he knew lots of sober New Hope people, and admired how fun and free they seemed to be. It wasn't long before he joined his sober friends and started going to AA meetings regularly. He began to change. No more lost cars, no more losing thousands at the casinos, less time at the gay baths in New York. He developed a real love and concern for others. I remember admiring him for that and the changes he was making. Whatever he was doing seemed to be working and it looked good to me.

Sometimes I'd tag along with him to meetings. Meanwhile I hadn't been drinking because of the support group rules, and actually *liked* it. But after the three, six week group sessions were over, I joined a friend on vacation for a couple of weeks in Key West. I hadn't planned to drink and I managed not to for several days but then one night, I just couldn't *not* drink—(double negative intended.)

The bartender was making a special drink and wouldn't take no for an answer. Well I guess she would have if I'd had the strength to resist but I caved and I kept caving. I'd say I *wasn't* and then I *would*. What was wrong with me? I could definitely stop drinking I just could not *stay stopped*. That's when I decided I better start going to the meetings and make an actual commitment not to drink.

I hadn't seen Jim in ages and then, out of the blue, there he was at a meeting.

'Good for him. Wow.' He'd been on a wild ride of his own. He'd barely skirted death several times. It was a miracle to see him at a meeting. We slowly began chatting again.

It was in Princeton where I met Pam, a friend of Marco's

at an ACOA, (Adult Child of Alcoholics,) meeting, a support meeting for friends and family of alcoholics.

Marco knew I was dating again and thought us a good match and she was. Pam was an attractive, dynamic woman, a successful executive and lots of fun. She had everything I wanted. We hit it off right from the beginning. We became fast friends *and* lovers. Our relationship was good but we seemed better as friends and we are even today, the best of friends.

Later, after the romantic part had dwindled, it was at a party at Pam's where I met Elaine, a well known executive for a large Philadelphia firm who was in a *serious* relationship with another woman. They had a child. I saw an affair, an opportunity for yet another relationship with no commitments. Old habits die hard. I could be *taken* but not possessed, *still* and I liked the unavailability.

Elaine was of a sort of female version of Woody Allen, more than appealing, for me she was *red hot*. Super butch, on the continuum Elaine was definitely 100 % gay. A little quirky and super smart, Elaine was recognized all over Philly, a celebrity of sorts. Our favorite date was the expense-account fancy lunch, followed by separating for a few hours and meeting up later at a hotel in Philly. I'd go ahead, prepare the room and myself and wait. I could barely open the door before she gently took total possession of me. Elaine was in control and that's how I liked it.

The magic began to dissipate some time later, after I got a small apartment in Philly. There is something about making the arrangements and, *sneaking* into a hotel. It was the *hiding* and the waiting, the different room every time. Not only was I beginning to lose interest, but some of my desire to be in a relationship with a woman was beginning to fade.

But there were others as well. I had several relationships over the next couple of years but something was always missing for me. The being with a woman was good, but I began to see that, of course I liked the sex and I liked the drama but I wasn't so sure about the lifestyle. I began to realize that my attraction, my need for a woman seemed to be that I literally ran to them for safety. I wanted them strong. Strong women, so different from my mother whom I perceived as so, so very weak. I was literally running to be saved, like I hadn't been as a child.

Maybe it's that I wasn't nurtured, didn't feel loved. Maybe it's because I wanted my mother to save me, to protect me. These women were strong and I was enormously attracted to that strength. Emotionally I was running to safety, just like I'd run to my mother for love and protection when my father was drinking. Even though there were limits to that love I would *still* run to her. I hadn't gotten what I needed as a child. I so wanted that loving female energy and strength.

My attractions are obviously complex. There are diverse acronyms for some sexual preferences—LGBTQ as in Lesbian, Gay, Bi-Sexual, Trans Gender, Queer. If there were one for me, I'm not sure what or how many letters would be needed to categorize me—*if* I felt the need to be categorized. I now understand that my attractions lie in three distinct but converging areas, Sexual, Emotional and Social.

Sexually, I realize I am attracted to both men and women with a preference for women.

Emotionally, I am strongly attracted to women. The sex is good but I've really never wanted a long-term relationship with a woman. I found I liked to experiment, play around, but just couldn't seem to take it seriously and I knew I *had* to make a choice. Just playing around with women didn't seem right and all the gay women I knew wanted long-term relationships.

Socially, I am very comfortable and enjoy being with a man. I had experimented and I knew this for sure. In the end it was Jim I had always wanted to be with. I *always* wanted that. but what have I done with my desire for women..When it comes up, and it does, I recognize it, I enjoy it, I have what

I call my *flirtations* which are seriously fun and at my age just the right thing.

One evening late in the summer, I was surprised when Jim gave me a call. He'd been curious about what I had been up to, wanting to share with me what was going on with him. I got to ask him about some of the things he'd been through before finding recovery. I listened and it wasn't pretty. Jim had reached a plateau, as well. He said he'd consumed all the drugs he could stand and hated the lifestyle.

The bigger miracle was that he wanted to change and was happy.

We chatted about where I'd been, my career, my escapades in the Hamptons, and how I'd gotten into the meetings. We would meet the following Friday night at Odette's for dinner, our old favorite place.

Dinner was wonderful and those old feelings of hope re-emerged. I had always wanted my relationship with him to be a good one; healthy, fun, not so crazy and stressful, what we never had. Could we have it? Was it ridiculous of me to even think it?

It was the using and everything that accompanies the using that got in the way. We agree to spend time together, work on our issues and share our growth. We both wanted to change.

We would help each other and we would continue to get help. Jim made a decision to go to rehab for twenty eight days. He wanted to do it 'right,' he said.

The last week of his rehab stint was reserved for family and I went. I learned so much about addictions and the addict's behavior that week. In other words I learned a lot about *myself* as well as about Jim. I became painfully aware that not all of our issues were Jim's alone. A lot of it was on me. It may be hard to believe, but "family week" at the rehab was an amazing experience. The closeness in the group among those attending was wonderful.

It was sometime during that week that I realized not only was I was not ready to return home but I was not ready to be with anyone, not Jim, not anyone, not yet. Old anger issues about Jim, our relationship, our past came up for me at family week at the rehab. I decided to remain at the rehab for two more weeks to come to terms with my resentments and anger. All of this touched something in me. Going immediately back into the relationship didn't feel right. I just couldn't jump back into my relationship with him.

So lots more work needed to be done, program work, like getting a sponsor, working the steps and going to meetings. As much as I needed the alcohol support group, as much as I knew I wanted a new life, it worried me at first, this getting sober permanently thing. What would my life be without drinking and partying. I expressed my concern to an old time member.

"Nothing will be the same, I'll be different."

"Good." She said.

I thought, 'How rude. She doesn't even know me. How does she know it will be an improvement.'

The truth is, no she didn't know me but she knew my type. I was no different from the rest of them, no better, and no worse. We all had so much in common and it wasn't only about wanting to stop drinking. I'd been on an emotional roller coaster for my entire life and, well, roller coasters just take you round and round. . . going nowhere.

No one decides early on in life, "Gee, I think I'll go to an alcohol support group when I get older." For most people it is *the most* dreaded option. I remember when I was younger and my food, wine and drug use made me feel crazy and declaring, "I will never ever go to a support group to stop drinking or go to any of those meetings." I saw the meetings as a last resort for only the worst of cases. After all I wasn't as bad as my *father*.

On the outside and to some people, I didn't look like I had a drinking problem. Friends were surprised when I stopped, but *I* knew. I knew the jig was up and had been for awhile. I couldn't drink anymore. It wasn't working for me. Actually it was making me depressed yet I couldn't *not drink* for more than a few weeks. I *did* need help.

Pain brings you into the twelve step rooms..To say it is *only* to stop drinking is putting it mildly. To say it is out of *pure desperate necessity* is more like it. And these recovery people seemed to be onto something.

Members of the group had diverse reasons for attending. Some might have lost their jobs and family. Others had lost everything, their family, their friends their jobs and their homes. They found themselves in places they should never have been, doing things they would never have done. These *were* desperate people. They came from every walk of life. More often than not these folks were just plain at home closet drinkers or bingers and given the times both drug and alcohol abusers.

Alcohol and drug abuse changes personalities dramatically over time. What used to make us feel better, more alive, more in control can begin to turn on us. With some, tempers flare uncontrollably, secrecy becomes the norm, and the once honest person now lies about his whereabouts and consumption. Neglected family members suffer. They no longer recognize their loved one as the loving person they once were.

As a matter of fact, they are often frightened and have been neglected, and *I knew that* for a fact.

As I look at it now I see I was bored, restless, and impulsive. I had an inability to tolerate stress. I was anxious, lonely and depressed. Who wouldn't drink with my background and with the stresses I had undergone? Who wouldn't drink if they had a family like mine?

Who wouldn't drink, *anyway?*

Didn't everyone drink? Forever, it seemed I'd switch around from Dramamine, to amphetamines, to pot, and Valium, and back to drinking. It's like the damn 'whack-a-mole' game at the fair. When one addiction gets whacked into submission, another pops up and then so on. . .

So, in not so many words, I came to realize that I was one of these people with their difficult, quirky, needy personalities. I had, in these groups, found like minded fellows whose background and personalities had driven them to drink. And all this time we thought we drank for fun. We were grandiose, forever declaring how dull the normal people were. Anyone would be dull compared to us, like being a *little dull* is so much worse than being a *mess.*

So, now that I had found my *tribe,* I had to see what was it these folks were doing that changed them for the better. I came to see it wasn't just the sobriety that made them healthier, happier, people; it was that they had truly given in and realized that they were not in control and they needed help. That was certainly true of their drinking, *that* they could absolutely not control. What else was out of their control? Well, it seems, a lot. The bills, the job, their health, the family were all out of their control, *everything.*

But I had my limits.

I had an ego and at that time, I was not fully willing to follow the program. It was suggested I needed to get a sponsor but not one to comply readily, I decided *that* was for *other* people. I wasn't about to share *my* innermost workings with someone else, nor was I going to talk about myself at meetings, having a *public persona* and all. I just couldn't. Other than going to meetings I didn't do many of the other things they told me to do either.

"Wasn't not drinking and going to meetings enough?

The philosophy of the group was a mystery to me at the time. Things like 'letting go and letting God' handle what I couldn't handle myself or 'keeping it simple.' I tailored the program to suit myself which isn't suggested.

I used the program as a workshop of sorts and taking on the saying, 'Take what you like and leave the rest,' to heart. So, I didn't do the program as 'prescribed.' I did it *my* way, incorporating into my life the things that appealed to me.

I didn't drink and I went to meetings. Those things I *could* do. I convinced myself that I could stay sober without a sponsor and without doing the steps. Would I make it?

And they persistently talked about *gratitude*. Gratitude, I had none. I was so preoccupied with my own issues I really didn't care about anyone else. I had no gratitude or appreciation for anyone. I was lost inside myself and my own confusing forest of feelings.

And yet, even though I wasn't really working the program the way it was recommended, the meetings made me feel great. I was definitely *not* a spokesperson for twelve step programs because really no one is but especially not someone like me, an unwilling semi-follower of sorts. But, the program gave me something I had never gotten before. I felt something I had never felt before. There was love in the rooms. I was no longer alone. Something was going on there for me. This child was finally being nurtured.

Today, many years later, I follow the program, "As prescribed." with pretty good success from lots of hard work and my Higher Power, the love and help of my sponsor and others in the program.

Jim and I were going to meetings both on our own and together. Life was changing for both of us. They say the program changes people. How would it change me? Could it do its magic on us as a couple

Together Again. I know, call me crazy, (and you wouldn't be the first. . .)

Jim and I were spending so much time together. It was beginning to feel silly keeping two houses going. A strong pull emerged to live together again. It felt safe. It felt real. And I was more in love with Jim than ever.

After searching for bit we found through our old friend, Mike Dyers, now a realtor, a wonderful cottage in the country, in Solebury, Pennsylvania, just outside of New Hope. The very dark green almost black, painted exterior blended in beautifully with the surrounding woods. The long wooded drive with just our house at the end, gave us the privacy we wanted and the stream behind made it even more charming.

Shortly after settling in at the house, Marco approached us, desperately seeking help for HAVANA. The bills were *huge*, the food purveyors refused to deliver and the partners were picking up provisions daily at Costco. The business fall-apart domino effect was uncontrollable. Tile after tile, the place was falling apart.

Would we buy in or better said, "Would we save the place?" We had the money, good reputations as chefs/restaurant people *and* we had the confidence. Only slightly crazy people with tons of confidence would be foolish enough to *pay* to take on such a mess but after working through it with lawyers, we came to an agreement and bought more than half of the shares for an excellent price.

After paying the taxes, the purveyors, cleaning up the joint in so many ways, Jim and I put into place a fresh, more appealing menu. As important as these changes were, the greatest priority was creating a new *corporate philosophy.*

We wanted HAVANA, and we put that in *capitals* always, to welcome to all sorts of people, young and old, gay and straight, families, singles, the executives on Harleys, (bikers who love riding beautiful River Road along the Delaware River in New Hope) artists and party people. The one thing we didn't want was the drug activity. Our considerable investment, our new found sobriety and clear headedness along with fear of legal ramifications helped us to see *clearly* the danger of allowing HAVANA to be one of the cornerstones of drug activity in New Hope.

That's where I come in. We are talking cocaine here. Before buying into the restaurant we pretty much knew everyone who sold and used, had waited in line for the bathrooms ourselves, stayed after hours and partied with them at the bar. So making these changes was *tricky* to say the least. Speaking to some directly I said, "Do all the drugs you want, just don't sell them here." Let's just say, a lot of the drug trade stopped. So did some of the bar patrons change but that was okay because the money in the till didn't suffer one bit. What *is* good to note is how Jim and I began to put into action our newfound consciousness and it felt so good to not only clean out our own houses but our new business as well.

A year after buying into HAVANA, our partner Marco was badly in need of a hernia operation, something he had put off for too long. The operation was a success at first but then he noticed that the incision just wasn't healing, not at all. The docs worked on it but still no healing. After a series of blood tests, it was confirmed—John was diagnosed with AIDS. This was 1986—he was the first person to have it in New Hope that we knew of. This was so *early* and so little was known. We were devastated and we knew we would do *anything* for him.

Shortly after the diagnosis, he began having difficulty breathing and was again admitted to the hospital where he immediately began to deteriorate. John was accepting everything that was happening to him—joyful and loving to the end. We, on the other hand, were beside ourselves with sadness. The medical staff stayed out of his room as much as possible and we felt he was being shunned. There were warning signs on his door and we were required to wear masks and gloves.

It wasn't more than a few weeks before the disease took him. We couldn't believe how quickly it happened. He was in an oxygen tank when we said our last goodbyes, *an oxygen tank.* . .

I leaned over to give him a kiss and said, "John, I will always love you. You are my brother, now and forever." He squeezed my hand. . . He was our best friend and now he was gone.

There were more than four hundred at the funeral. He was so loved.

Six months after his passing I felt the strong pull to help Hyacinth, the local AIDS organization in memory of John. My friend Steve and I planned it together. After meeting with the Hyacinth board, it was decided we would ask fifteen local restaurant chefs if they would join us in the event hosted by Odette's. Hors D'oeuvre stations were set up throughout the restaurant featuring signature appetizers. Local musicians played and bartenders volunteered to make drinks. More than three hundred attended, contributing a good amount of money in John's name. He would have been enormously proud.

After John died, two more of New Hope's restaurant owners died. Then as time went on we lost more. The grief was unbearable. One day, some years later, I made a list of all of our friends and acquaintances we had lost, taking the time to grieve and pray for each one. The closest were John and our old friend and restaurant manager, Tom Thorpe. My count was up to thirty five.

When we and by that I mean *everyone* lost so many lovely, creative, beautiful people in what seemed like a very short time, we lost so much. Those of us who knew them well experienced a kind of grieving usually reserved for older people. We lost our friends and loved ones so young and en mass. Nothing would ever be the same nor would we. The sanctity of life was never clearer to me. Where I once had no gratitude or appreciation, I was now overwhelmed by it. Our friends now seemed more precious than ever, while those we lost would never be forgotten. We would defend them forever to those who chose not to understand or grieve with us.

Now we were the sole owners of the restaurant. I knew when we bought the restaurant that from that point on our life would be on display. We were 'out there.' A restaurateur's private life seems to be everyone's business. I don't know why but that's the way it is.

I found myself becoming a public personality, an entertainer of sorts. Owning a restaurant and being out front greeting the people, making everyone happy, we became like actors. I had developed more of a *persona*, a very positive persona. Jim and I both had a way of making people feel comfortable and welcome which was perfect considering that the philosophy was to *welcome* everyone, in the first place. It wasn't until I started to feel better about myself after having been sober for a while that I felt on the inside just like what I was presenting on the outside. I guess the role-playing helped. I know they say if you don't feel great, if you don't feel happy, act as if.

Act as if you are this positive person and you know what eventually you will be. It works.

Running the place was a wonderful, rewarding experience in so many ways yet so outrageously stressful. So even with this *positive persona* of mine I wasn't always at my best and I wasn't always my best especially when something went awry at the restaurant. Jim and I wanted the restaurant to be a certain way, *our way*, our vision and every day we had to rein it in. I had to tell the employees what to do all the time and it wore on me. I could hear the exasperation in my voice and I knew they did as well. I sounded mean I guess.

At some point when meeting with a spiritual advisor about this, she said,

"You need to take the fear out of your voice."

Fear? Was it fear, of what? And then I got it. Revelation. . . I wasn't secure in my power. It was then I realized that I could calmly and pleasantly show them what was needed if I no longer felt guilty. On some level, I felt I had no right to tell them what to do. I began to see that as the owner of the restaurant I had the right to be the boss. The problem was that I had gone from being an employee who worked and played with these people for years to being their employer. I had been so concerned about what they thought of me. It was so difficult to boss my friends. When I began to own my power as the owner, the one with the vision and the right to exercise it, everything changed with my relationship with the employees.

There is nothing like owning a restaurant and especially a bar. It's like attending an over the top grad school specializing in 'crazy.' It has been my observation that people from dysfunctional families are drawn to the restaurant business. My own family dysfunction had made me an *expert* in a crisis. Give me a dire situation and I *will* handle it, no problem. It's *later* after everything is back to normal that I fall apart.

In the past, I had many times put myself and others in situations that had been unsafe. Now I had a group of recovery friends who had been down the same road or a similar path. They realized the risks they taken, although fun at one time, were no longer an option.

So now I was in a new way of life, a life Jim and I could lead together. Yet we were placing ourselves in a business that was *notorious* for risk. And we had to become *serious* people running a *serious* business, dodging all those things we had *relished* for so long.

We had come full circle. Always cautious amid my riskier friends, more than ever I had to become a watchdog.

The restaurant became everything to us. It was our creativity and we had a lot of it. It was our livelihood and with more than thirty employees at the time, a big responsibility. So many were so loyal and so good. We helped them when they were sick like our good friend Tom and others. We were with these employees to the end. Pay checks were paid whether they worked or not. It was our duty and our pleasure, to do the right thing. There is nothing like it.

When people hear we owned a restaurant they invariably say,

"That's a tough business."

I feel like saying, "You're preaching to the choir."

They have no clue. Tough, 'oh yes it is.' The restaurant was a huge success but getting there was rough. The business experienced financial stress every winter when it snowed every weekend and every spring when it rained all season or after major floods. Sometimes we didn't know if we'd make it at all. But we did, we survived and literally thrived, bit by bit, year by year. And so did Jim and I as a couple. I had finally come to some resolve regarding my sexuality. We were clear headed and successful. Life was good, not perfect but good.

But this tale is *not* over. I'm still alive aren't I? We both are. So what has happened since Jim and I got into recovery and bought the restaurant? After the AIDS crisis had its very intense impact on our lives, *so* much happened.

The Business. . .

Jim and I grew the restaurant over time, adding on another building making it one of the largest, busiest restaurants/bars between Philadelphia and New York with more than 100 employees whose loyalty and hard work made all of this possible.

HAVANA was a Mecca for the fun crowd and the stories—you would not believe.

In a Family Way. . .

In the beginning of our relationship Jim and I wanted children but it never happened back then and for many years we didn't give it another thought, and that's a good thing. But later, with our lives being more stable and our biological clocks clicking we looked to adopt.

My cousin John called one evening telling us to turn on the TV. "20/20 is airing a program on the orphanages in Romania. These children need adopting."

We were astonished by what we saw on TV that night. The obviously malnourished children seemed to be living in what looked more like prisons than orphanages. Babies and toddlers warehoused in wall-to-wall cribs, sad-eyed and painfully thin, they continuously nurtured them-selves by rocking for comfort. Understanding their need to rock themselves in their cribs to nurture themselves rocked me. . .

Seeing this struck us in a way we had never felt before. Jim and I wept and wept. We had to do this.

We did. We adopted a child, a tiny little girl almost seven years old from Romania. Nadia looked to be four, had lived in abject poverty with her mother and abusive alcoholic father and seven siblings until she was five, in a one room, falling down, thatched cottage with half the roof missing until she was taken to an orphanage at age six. She and several other children in the family had been placed in orphanages or given up for adoption because the parents were incapable of taking care of them.

Nadia was one of the last children adopted from Romania in the 1991. She knew nothing of life as we know it. Everything was so new and different for her in America, the abundance we take for granted, our home, a new language, new parents, school and of course the *grieving*. Nadia had already been through so much and now she found her little self with a new set of situations to go through, everything a person can experience, really.

Although she took to us immediately and loved us from the beginning, she still had to get to know us, understand and feel comfortable in her new life, process her emotions, learn the culture into which she had been thrown. She had to become a student of *everything* and I mean *everything;* the language, how to make friends with the American kids her age despite the fact that they were so far ahead of her in school. She started in nursery school at seven and was almost impossibly far behind. It was a very deep and intense struggle for her from the start. Nadia at almost seven, had never seen book, never held a pencil, had no idea about numbers, the names of colors or drawing and although she had been taken care of as a baby she had not been nurtured after that.

What she left behind, we wouldn't think of as much, but the loss was unbearable. I was her new, unknown, adoptive mother and Jim, the new, very loving father. I cannot imagine the confusion and pain she must have been in and just how strange everything must have seemed.

I was this mother, *who had not been nurtured*, who knew the importance of nurturing. It is no wonder I was so touched by the love and nurture deprived orphans rocking themselves. I seemed to have come full circle. I, more than most, could understand and help this sweet, adorable, loving, sad child. Having not been rocked, I rocked her, having not been held, I held her. I loved her.

Jim loved her. He always said, "If we love her she will heal."

And we did and she loved us right back—along with the sadness, there was great love and joy, for her and for us. We became parents, very good parents, at least we did our best but we had our own challenges.

THE LESSONS. . .

I have learned so much putting pen to paper the things that have happened, how it affected me and who I have become. This writing is one of the most powerful things I have ever done and I will never be the same, and that's a *good* thing.

What kept me writing for all these months more than anything was the hope that I might help in some way those who are lost, who are trying to make sense of the life they have been given and those who like me had to make it up as they went along until they *finally* found a clue.

There *is* hope.

It doesn't matter what our past issues were and I had many: neglect, abuse, addiction, anxiety, family dysfunction, Post Traumatic Stress Disorder and sexuality issues. Many are lost. I was lost. How was I to find the family and friends I so longed for? Where was love, the nurturing and acceptance? How would I ever feel at peace, have serenity and sobriety? How was I ever going to shake this *pain*?

Even as a child, I thought the only way out was through escape and believe me, I tried. Whether escaping to the bowels of the Queen Mary at four, knocking myself out by Dramamining my way to Florida in the back of my parents car, speedily zipping through my 'tween years on food and amphetamines and later smoking pot until I crashed, to find the only escape left was drinking and of course the occasional cocaine.

As I see it, we are all survivors, survivors of something. Before that we were victims. Of course, I was a victim as a child. Today I am only a victim to the extent of my own immaturity, dysfunction and unwillingness to feel the pain, forgive others, move on and look at my own part in everything. I have come to see the way out is not through escape. It is by going straight through the eye of it. Avoidance, a once useful tool no longer works for me.

These *many* years later, I have a sponsor, I go to meetings, I sponsor and try to be of service to others. Jim, my friends, my recovery groups, dependence on my Higher Power, the things I have learned and of course trial and error have given me a gratitude and confidence which I could only have dreamed.

So, I now share my story.

May those who seek, find.

May those in pain find a way to heal.

The meaning of life
is to find your gift.
The purpose of life
is to give it away."

— PABLO PICASSO

"Sometimes you don't realize
the weight of something
you've been carrying,
until you feel the weight
of its release."

— UNKNOWN

Made in the USA
Middletown, DE
19 September 2019